GRADE CLEANSE

FROM THE POWER OF ICU LEARNING LIBRARY

THE GRADE CLEANSE

A ROADMAP TO HEALTHY GRADING

Challenge Conventional Grading Practices
and Gather Practical Strategies to
Cultivate Grades that Reflect Learning

DANNY HILL
GARNET HILLMAN

The Grade Cleanse
Danny Hill
Garnet Hillman

Power of ICU
102 Hartman Drive
Suite G #224
Lebanon, Tennessee 37087

www.poweroficu.com

Copyeditor: Kelly Skipworth
Collaborators: Amy Wood, Katie Budrow, Tory Atwood, Kirk Humphreys,
        Jason Ozbolt, Vicki Hines
Production Editor: Clayton Ledford

ISBN: 978-0-9856961-7-7

Our Healthy Grade Litmus Test

A healthy grade reflects what a student has learned in relation to an academic standard based on most recent and consistent evidence.

TABLE OF CONTENTS

A⁺

PART 3: ALIGNING INSTRUCTION, PRACTICE, AND ASSESSMENT

GRADE CLEANSE

FOREWORD

I met Danny Hill last year when he came to my school to present his "proven formula for student success," *The Power of ICU*. Our school quickly adopted the ICU approach, and by the beginning of summer vacation, EVERY student had completed EVERY assignment. Furthermore, attendance increased, student attitudes improved, and students developed a new understanding about how much we truly cared about them as individuals. Our next challenge as a staff is to continue to improve the quality of our assignments and the health of our grades.

When Danny asked me to work with him and his coauthor Garnet Hillman by offering feedback on their ideas and by editing their book, it was an honor for me because these two professionals are the epitome of excellence in education. In *Grade Cleanse*, Garnet and Danny ask us to take an honest look at our current grading habits and encourage us to replace them with **healthier**, research-based methods to improve student success.

A few years ago, I embarked on a professional journey that would change my teaching forever. I separated behaviors from grades, deconstructed my standards, and created folders so that students could color code their progress. These changes have had a positive impact on student achievement because my students now know how well they have mastered each learning target at any given time.

At some point in my journey, I concluded that the next step was outside my comfort zone. I realized that using four proficiency levels with my students (although very effective), would not yield accurate marking period grades in my school's online gradebook. *Grade Cleanse* has helped me let go of the fear and move forward. Their approach of taking baby steps along with the freedom to make mistakes are refreshing themes in this book.

One of the most powerful chapters in *Grade Cleanse* addresses the need to immerse our students in the **language of learning**. If we desire healthier grading practices, we must constantly encourage our students to **move up** a level and to do practice and more practice to get there. The language that we use in our classroom can completely change the culture. Eventually, students will no longer be asking how many points they received or what grade they earned. Rather, they will be asking if they met the learning target or if they need more practice. Discussions about homework will be replaced with conversations about practice, and students will be motivated intrinsically as they move up, one level at a time.

To some of you, the ideas set forth in *Grade Cleanse* might seem quite revolutionary because they ask you to look at grading in a whole new way and to let go of non-essential methods that do not maximize student achievement. To others who have already embarked on a journey to make grades more meaningful, this book will leave you refreshed and determined to keep going.

Let's face it. Teachers constantly feel the pressure of state testing, rigorous standards, additional expectations, added initiatives, new information, ever-changing technology, and the list goes on. Sometimes it can feel overwhelming. **For me, *Grade Cleanse* is a welcome relief because it takes me back to the beginning, declutters my mind, and helps me focus on what is truly important: student success.**

Kelly Skipworth
Green High School
Franklin Furnace, Ohio

PREFACE
CLEANSING GRADING PRACTICES

When you look into a glass of water, what do you see? Preferably, what you see would be clear without any sediment or discoloration. When we consider grades, this *clarity* is what we desire as well. However, many times we are looking at a glass of *mud*. At first glance, we may not realize the muddiness in our practices, yet consider the following: There are so many factors contributing to grades that seeing through the glass is virtually impossible. The grade is a muddy mess comprised of academic achievement, behaviors, and growth. We want grades to be clear, but when used in a traditional sense, they are far from transparent.

Cleansing grading practices involves taking a hard look at *why* we grade, *how* we grade, and *what* impact our grades have on the culture of our classroom and school. We need to take the mud and replace it with clear water. Cleansing grading practices demands that all essential information about student achievement is separate from *behaviors*. When this happens, grades have clarity, and we can use them to enhance student learning. This is difficult work but incredibly rewarding. By cleansing grades, we are able to increase the accuracy of reporting and have a lasting impact on the culture of our school and classroom. This cleanse provides students with the opportunity to focus on what is truly important—learning.

A good friend was named principal of a new, large high school and was given the opportunity to hire his entire staff. Having been a very popular assistant principal, many of the best teachers in the district and neighboring districts applied. Near the end of each interview, he asked every candidate this question: "What is the purpose of a grade?" He called me one day following a full day of interviews and said, "Nobody knows the purpose of a grade. These are some of the best teachers, and I cannot wait to work with them, but I have only had two teachers even come close to mentioning that grades should reflect student learning. I hear a lot of explanation of their point system, how many grades they take, and how they weigh daily work and tests. Several teachers just seemed stumped. One really good teacher just admitted, 'You know, I really haven't given it much thought. Can I go home and study it?'" My friend said several candidates called him a day or two later and asked for another chance to respond.

I can relate. I used to spend a lot of time trying to explain my grading system to my students. I would put numbers on the board and show them how one low grade averaged in would lower their overall average significantly. "Be sure to study hard for every test. Turn in your folder and assignments on time because one low grade destroys your final average." Instead of rethinking our approach, my colleagues and I shared a variety of grade massaging quick-fixes including dropping the lowest grade, curving grades, and giving students no less than a 60. This universally accepted grading scheme was to increase the number of grades so a zero or low grade would not count as much. I did the best I could at the time, but my grades were meaningless.

According to Doug Reeves, founder of The Leadership and Learning Center, "Giving grades that are inflated with non-academic points or deflated due to poor behaviors produce inaccurate results. Giving students and parents inaccurate feedback is counter-productive."

When we were students, we earned points, and those translated to a letter grade. The points came from everything—tests, quizzes, homework, classwork, participation, extra credit, compliance, behaviors, etc. The *final grade* was some sort of magical compilation of those things with different weights and values.

As we transitioned to being teachers, we continued this practice by carefully considering how many points each assignment and assessment would be worth. We graded and entered everything because we just didn't know better. We believe that many educators are in the same place today and have never taken the opportunity to reflect on their grading practices. This is not something that comes up in teacher preparatory coursework at the university level or in discussions throughout most clinical experiences. Most never even consider that there is a better way to grade than what has always been done.

What makes grading such a stagnate practice that has not changed in the past 100+ years? Kids have changed, learning has changed, instructional practice has changed, the workforce has changed, our curriculum is now standard specific, and yet grading remains the same.

Thomas Guskey, an expert in evaluation design, analysis, and educational reform, asks, "Do our grades for students reflect the degree to which they have met the standards for a course?"

Why call it a "cleanse?" We think this will help you view this as an opportunity rather than an assignment—an opportunity to cleanse your grading of unhealthy practices like combining student behaviors with academics and playing the "points game" with grades. Cleansing our grades is much like cleansing our bodies. We need to take a look at what we are putting *in* and what we are getting *out* of the process. With health, we want to ensure we get the most out of our food (what we put in), in order to be healthy, fit, and feeling good (what we get out). With grades, the same is true. We want to put in clear parameters for what belongs in a grade (what we put in), so our grades will be meaningful and accurate (what we get out).

Our **Grade Cleanse** will take your grading practices from muddy to clear. This is a "how to" resource for you to create healthy grading practices that are clear not only to you but also to parents and students. Simple steps are provided that can be implemented to focus students and classrooms on learning rather than grades.

Our unique approach allows you to move at your own pace. There are a series of challenges, or "how-to," baby steps, that give teachers time to *think*, resulting in a change in mindset and excitement. **Cleanse One** asks you to analyze what makes up a grade and move forward with changes that will make them more accurate, transparent, and meaningful. Cleansing behaviors out will naturally improve the health of academic grades.

Throughout our cleanse, we will fill your mind with healthy nutrients of *grading truth* from experts and practitioners. These truths will free you up to let go of time-consuming, wasteful (yet widely accepted) grading practices. Your intrinsic motor will be fueled by significantly improved student motivation and learning.

PART ONE

CLEANSING BEHAVIORS FROM ACADEMIC GRADES: ESTABLISHING LANGUAGE THAT IS LEARNING FOCUSED

"I think I have cut out giving 'points' for behaviors. I do give 'extra points' to students who study at home with their parents. Is that wrong? I just feel like it should 'count for something' if they put in the extra time to study at home."

Separating behaviors from grades seems easy at first glance. However, cleaning up our grading mess takes time and careful analysis. Feeling "it" should count for *something* is not wrong or bad. The question is, "Does 'it' belong in the academic grade?" Be patient with the cleanse and carefully examine everything, including what "feels right" before allowing anything to remain in your healthy, academic grade category.

Consider this analogy. Think about a second grader's desk. When you peer in (unless it is the first day of school), there is a messy combination of books, papers, folders, pencils, erasers, markers, and the list goes on. I have had this experience with my own children, and glancing inside makes me wonder how they could possibly find anything or know the entire contents! Looking at the desk from the outside, you wouldn't necessarily know the chaos that lies within. All sorts of things can hide in the desk, and yet it maintains this outward appearance of organization and simplicity. My sons have claimed numerous times that books, assignments, and school supplies are lost.

"Lost" seems to be the code word for missing in the chasm of the desk. Then the day arrives for desk clean-out. Amazingly, the lost items are found. Letter grades are just like these desks—nice neat packages hiding something very chaotic inside. With grading, we put all sorts of pieces like weights, categories, behaviors, assignments, and assessments into letter grades.

Behaviors and growth get lost in what appears to be solely an academic mark. The look of the desk from the outside, just like the letter grade, isn't telling us the whole story. What lies within is a mess. Now is the time to clean out the messy desk of grading, sort out everything that makes up the grade, and do a major clean-out. Let's tidy up this mess for the sake of accuracy in reporting, and more importantly, for the sake of student learning and motivation. We recommend that you view each cleanse as a *baby step* forward.

Before beginning the cleanse, we must answer *What is the purpose of grading?* In the most simplistic sense, grades serve as a piece of communication. According to author and respected grading expert, Rick Wormeli, "We need to change the metaphor: Grades are not rewards, affirmation, validation, or compensation. They are communication; that's it." They communicate academic achievement...or do they? We would like to think so, but when all things are considered, many behaviors and non-academic factors have found their way into our grading paradigm. These factors have become part of grading norms over the years and have been left out of our discussion.

For many elementary schools, reporting behaviors separately from academic grades is fairly routine. Once students get to middle and high school, every teacher has a different grading system, and most include behaviors like compliance, following rules, participation, effort, etc. along with the demonstration of learning. Teachers tell students, "It is your responsibility to keep up with my grading system," which is chaotic for our students. Students are expected to "figure out" each teacher and keep up with a half-dozen different schemes;

it's exhausting. Too many students just shut down and refuse to play the game of school. Even those students who play the game well have lost their focus. School is about learning, not chasing points or percentages. If student success truly is our main purpose, then our fragmented approach to grades must be replaced with harmony and synchronization as students move from teacher to teacher.

I have heard our present traditional grading system referred to as a "poisonous soup" where educators have routinely dumped everything. Have you been taught, "Everything must be graded?" The status quo approach to teaching responsibility is to grade it. If this is working, then why is student apathy and irresponsibility still a major problem? How to handle dishonesty? Add it into the student's grade. How to handle a lack of engagement? "It matters," so toss it into the grade. Students not being timely with their work? You guessed it—figure it into the grade. Does an "A" mean that Emily has learned the material or that she is good at playing the game of school? What about a "C"? Does Katherine have some gaps in proficiency, or is she chronically late with her assignments? Before you get started with the first cleanse, keep in mind that **our goal is not** *perfect grading*, **which is not possible, but** *healthy grading*, **which is attainable and realistic.**

So you are saying there are no consequences for turning in work late? Many of you are already familiar with Power of ICU (www. poweroficu.com) and our extremely successful approach to missing assignments and late work. The consequence for not turning in an assignment is that the student still has to complete the assignment on *their time*. Before school, instead of hanging out with their friends, students on the ICU list complete missing assignments in the ICU room where extra help is available. During lunch, they attend a *working lunch* to complete or redo an assignment. After school, they complete assignments with the help of teachers and peer mentors. Every minute of down time during the school day and school year is used for students to complete assignments outside the classroom.

Instead of threatening and rewarding students, ICU offers a different and highly effective approach that builds upon intrinsic motivation. *Brick House*, by Danny Hill, details the steps to build a strong infrastructure with several layers of support so that teachers are no longer left alone to deal with student apathy and responsibility. The *ICU Database* sends immediate text messages and emails to parents informing them of any missed assignment to help prevent a student from falling behind. We believe all three parts of the ICU formula are necessary to develop a culture of learning in your school:

Completion

+

Quality Assignments/Assessments

+

Healthy Grading

=

Student Success

CLEANSE NUMBER ONE
CAN I CLEANSE BEHAVIORS FROM ACADEMIC GRADES?

"...in our offices and our classrooms we have way too much compliance and way too little engagement. The former might get you through the day, but only the latter will get you through the night."

-Daniel Pink

At the beginning of my teaching career, I did what had been done to me and what I had done throughout my student teaching. I included behaviors as a "normal" part of students' grades. Growing up, this was standard practice in the classroom, and I knew nothing different. Once I began teaching, I had a lot of support in this endeavor—nothing amiss in my evaluations from administration, peers who respected what I was doing in my classroom, and quiet students who were compliant. People would walk by my classroom and not blink an eye. But to be honest, I was very harsh. I had grading policies that included a variety of behaviors. Late work was not accepted and went into the grade book as a zero. I gave points for participation in class. As embarrassing as this is, extra credit was awarded for bringing in tissues at the beginning of the year, food for the food drive, and reading books off a provided list. Students even earned points for things like getting their syllabus signed at the beginning of the year. What I hadn't considered was how much these practices were hindering the learning in my classroom.

Counting behaviors as part of the grade was affecting my students in two different ways. One group, the "compliant" students, were into "point collection" and were disengaged from their learning in order to gather enough for the grade they wanted. The other group had "checked out" because they knew they could not keep up with the point system. Both groups were distracted from learning in my classroom—the exact opposite of what I wanted. Responsibility was taught through these practices, or at least I thought it was. I was a subscriber to the sentiment, "If I don't grade it, they won't do it." Including non-academic behaviors in my grades wasn't producing the desired results, but I never batted an eye or reflected on the practice. Grades for behaviors, such as whether they turn in an assignment or participate in class, don't have anything to do with a student's learning or demonstration of proficiency of learning targets.

Grades have been used to punish students for being tardy, turning assignments in late, cheating, etc. for years. If you take this tool away from teachers, they are going to "freak out."

Separating non-academic behaviors from academic grades does not mean you throw your school-wide or classroom discipline plan out the window. Cheating, tardies, severe behaviors, plus the three D's (disrupt, disobey, and disrespect) all fall under every *discipline code* which, of course, is still in effect. Cleansing grading practices opens the door for teachers to use common sense when they grade. Do you believe grades should be used as a "tool" or "weapon" to punish students? If something isn't related to the subject matter, then it doesn't belong in the grade. Keep it simple! The categories, weights, and point values used in traditional grading add a lot of non-essentials to teachers' plates. There is a lot of figuring that teachers, students, and parents have to do to understand just how much academics and behaviors have each contributed to the letter grade. Simplify your practices and remove behaviors from the grade. Allow the grade to communicate learning.

Late work is probably the most common behavior included in grades. The practice of lowering academic grades because something is turned in late has been the status quo for quite some time. Teachers want to make sure they are holding students accountable for deadlines and feel the only way to do this is to include it in the grade. Is "meets deadlines" one of your academic standards? What does turning in something on time have to do with a reading standard? Timeliness is important, but it must be reported separately. And don't forget the ICU approach: "The consequence for not completing a quality assignment is that you still have to complete it on your *own time* (before, during, or after school)."

So please don't "freak out." Negative, extrinsic motivators that "stick" students with lost points and/or a lower grade have no long-term positive results, just as positive, extrinsic motivators like the "carrot" or "bribe" for additional points and/or a higher grade exhaust the teacher and result in no long-term gain. Think band-aid!

One school recently appointed a Grade Analysis Team. This team of great thinkers was given the task of examining and reporting to the staff on the following:

1. A list of everything being included in student grades at their school.

2. What challenges they foresee in making changes to grading practices?

Here are some comments from the team after their analysis:

- *"I realized how much pressure I feel to hand the parents a certain number of grades so they will not complain. Many of them check the electronic grade book and get upset if there aren't several grades for their child."*

- *"Parents get mad when their child does not have at least one grade per week. In fact, I am pretty sure it is a district policy to have at least one grade per subject for each child a week."*

- *"We all agree with giving extra practice, extra time, and extra help to students who need it. But, when we know parents will complain if there is nothing in the electronic grade book for a week it becomes very stressful, not a simple fix."*

- *"I think everyone is starting to 'look at' grades differently. It takes a lot of time."*

- *"One teacher drops the lowest grade, another does not. One teacher grades daily work, another does not. One teacher uses percentages, another does not. One thing we all agree on is that 'dysfunctional' is the best way to describe our grading practices."*

What can be done? Do your students know for sure that you are pulling for them to succeed? This is huge. We need to reflect on *intrinsic* motivators proven to have long-term, positive results. For example, positive relationships, frequent conversations, and goal setting are powerful motivators. Simply saying you are pulling for your students is not enough. The students must know it for sure. Punishment with grades says "gotcha" to your students and doesn't change behavior. Thomas Guskey, a well respected grading expert, says, "Too many teachers rely on using grades as their weapon of last resort." If this worked, all the students that got a zero on an assignment would complete every one after that. We're not sure about everyone else, but this never happened for us!

The challenges for **Grade Cleanse One** are simple and effective ways to begin clearing up our muddy grading waters and improve the accuracy in our reporting. Analysis invigorates and leads to discovery, which energizes. **Being transparent throughout the cleanse is very important.** Throw your thinking in the air and seize this "move-at-your-own-pace" opportunity to audit established grading practices, which hopefully will change your approach. Give yourself permission to let go of behavioral reporting and communicate it separately.

"Some of us think holding on makes us strong, but sometimes it is letting go."

-Hermann Hesse

CHALLENGE ONE

AUDIT GRADING PRACTICES

Instructions for Required Action Steps

- **List:** Record all factors that have been or are currently incorporated into grades.

- **Sort:** Which of those factors are academic and which are non-academic? *Here is where using sticky notes will make it easier.*

- **Ask:** What are some of the most bizarre items from the lists?

- **Consider:** Why have non-academic factors been included with academics in calculating a student's grade?

Audit: To inspect, examine, survey, go through, scrutinize, check, probe, verify, analyze, appraise, "to give something the once over."

Strategy: In small groups of teachers, create a list of all factors that contribute to grades. These can be ones they have included, have been included by others, or were included in their grades when they were in school. Put each one on a sticky note—one item per note. After brainstorming, take all the sticky notes and sort them into two categories: academic and non-academic.

Once the sticky notes have been separated, have a discussion about why those have been included, and have fun with the bizarre ones! This is a very effective and simple in-service experience for the entire faculty, grade level teams, or departments.

Strategy (student involvement): Ask students, "What is the weirdest thing you have ever received a grade for?" This question will stimulate lots of energy and help get them started. Instead of responding out loud, tell them to write all of their responses on sticky notes and place them at the center of their table. Next, instruct them to record everything they can think of that teachers include in their grades. Be sure to let them think on their own and not comment on anything you see or hear (Socratic) at this point. Ask for each group to share their top one or two craziest things ever graded, and let it go on as long as they are having fun. Ask them, "Why do you find these things crazy or weird?" This activity can be done in any classroom, but it is wise to coordinate this with other teachers so that it is not repeated several times for students.

Hopefully the discussion will lay the foundation for students to separate the academic sticky notes from the non-academic ones. After each group has brainstormed and separated the behaviors, have the kids share with the group. As a group, talk about why the separation is important. Discuss why this separation is a good thing and what it tells us. When they do the hands-on separation of academics and behaviors, they may want to give their opinions of what a healthy grade should include.

Using Socratic questioning (you stay neutral), try some of these questions, and allow for the discussion to remain open-ended. Have all students stand in the center of the room. As soon as you read the question and without any discussion, have students who agree move to one side of the room and those that disagree move to the opposite side of the room. Neutral is an acceptable position also, and moving throughout the discussion is fine if they change their minds.

Agree or disagree:

- I believe the grades I receive in school reflect what I have learned.
- When a student gets an A in a course, that means he/she learned the material.
- My parents emphasize grades more than learning.

Other statements/questions to generate energized discussion:

- If my teacher told me at the beginning of a course that I would receive an "A" even if I never came to class, did any assignments, or took any tests, would I put in less effort, the same amount of effort, or more effort?
- Do colleges care more about your grade point average or your ACT/SAT score? Why?

Doing an audit of grading practices reveals a lot about our grades and how they are muddy. Until we took a hard look at what we used in our grade books, we had no idea how many behaviors had found their way in. Once we audited our practices and identified what needed to go, the grades took a huge step forward in their health.

Here is a list of some common and not so common behaviors that have found their way into academic grades.

- Timeliness
- Perseverance
- Participation
- Attendance/tardiness
- Compliance with rules
- Homework completion
- Creativity
- Following directions
- Neatness

More bizarre behaviors included in grades:

- Bringing in supplies
- Contributing food for the food drive
- Dressing up for a presentation
- Coloring

- Bringing in bottle caps for free music (yes, this one did happen)
- Getting forms/agendas signed

Be sure to create an open forum so that everyone will honestly contribute all "grading practices," whether or not they have used them. This activity is not about placing blame; it is about gaining clarity in our practices. The more honest all participants are able to be, the more valuable this experience becomes. This is not about judgment; it is an opportunity to change our thinking. Remember, we didn't think that our grading was that muddied by other factors, but it definitely was. Once we became aware of a different approach, we kept thinking, "How did all these non-academic factors creep into the mix? What were we thinking?"

Rick Stiggins, founder and executive director of the ETS Assessment Training Institute, strongly believes, "Inaccurate data leads to counterproductive instructional decisions, and thus it is harmful to students."

Challenge One should inspire you to voluntarily remove non-academic items from your grading routine. Taking into account everything that was listed academically, teachers can now visualize what should be contributing to a student's grade. Reflecting on this list and removing non-academics leads to healthier grading.

Reflect:

_____

_____

_____

_____

_____

CHALLENGE TWO

DISCUSS AND DECIDE UPON THREE TO SIX NON-ACADEMIC BEHAVIORS THAT WILL BENEFIT TEACHERS, PARENTS, AND STUDENTS THE MOST WITH REGARD TO REPORTING

Teachers will not want to purge certain behaviors from their grades without a replacement strategy!

We agree. That is where Cleanse One is taking you, so be patient and stay with it. We know that changing grading practices can be painful. That is why we are offering a slow cleanse that gives everyone time to think and process. These baby steps are less painful than the usual "quick fix" approach that overwhelms and often blows up with no lasting improvement.

Instructions for Required Action Steps

- **State:** Positive behaviors and habits are very important. However, they absolutely must be separated from academic achievement in order to cleanse our practices and improve the quality and accuracy of grades.

- **Decide:** Which of these non-academic factors are important enough to report to parents and students? Which are keepers?

Strategy: Take all the sticky notes with behaviors on them from Challenge One, and spread them out so all can be clearly seen. Look for overlap and similarities between them, and eliminate any that are close to the same. The next step is to determine which behaviors would be included on a report to parents and students. If you were a parent, what would you want to know about your child's work habits?

Which behaviors are most important as your child moves through his or her school years and beyond? Are there some on the list that would be difficult to report on? Keep weaning the list down until you arrive at three to six behaviors.

Strategy (student involvement): Can the students determine which behaviors will be reported? The short answer is—yes. Take the behaviors that students previously brainstormed, eliminate similar behaviors, and create a gallery walk. Put each behavior on a piece of paper around your room, and have the kids walk around and vote on which behaviors should be used for reporting. Students get three votes: They can put a "+" sign on three of the papers, but no more. Tally up the votes, and go from there!

Selecting certain behaviors to be used for reporting does not mean that these are the only ones emphasized in the classroom. As educators, we are working with students to help them develop the habits that will serve them well in future schooling and their adult lives. The ones selected for reporting should be assessable, meaning teachers should be able to collect data and make a determination of how often or how well the student displays the behavior. There are some behaviors that are very difficult, if not impossible, to assess—one example being *effort*. Teachers cannot determine with accuracy how often or how well students are displaying effort—this is something that is only truly known by the students themselves. A behavior that is similar, but assessable, is *perseverance*. Teachers can plainly see when students persevere in their learning, and don't give up until they "get it."

From primary through secondary school, educators consistently emphasize treating one another with respect, kindness, and always honesty. Everyone agrees that student work habits and behaviors are very important. Their behaviors are the means by which they grow academically; they are how the students work, interact with others, and self-manage. Be a role model for your students. Show them what it looks like to be respectful, responsible, and trustworthy.

Never forget that we are not perfect—teachers and students alike. Making a mistake is part of being human, and kids need to be reminded of that fact. More importantly, we must turn our mistakes into opportunities to learn.

Remember, <u>including the reporting of behaviors with academic grades has been routine because behaviors do need to be reported, and there has been no alternative tool to separate them</u>. In this part of the cleanse, decide which behaviors we can accurately observe, provide feedback for, and report to students and parents. Most teachers will choose a minimum of three and a maximum of six, but the number is up to you.

Challenge Two should put you at ease when separating behaviors from the academic grade by providing a place to report behaviors and habits. Doing so creates a platform for parents to clearly know where students' strengths and areas of growth lie regarding their classroom behaviors. Parents want to know this information, and clarity is lost when behaviors are lumped into a single grade. The separation allows parents to help their students be successful not only with their academics, but also with their behaviors.

Reflect:

_____

_____

_____

_____

_____

_____

CHALLENGE THREE

DEVELOP A FORMAT TO GIVE FEEDBACK AND REPORT BEHAVIORS - EXCLUSIVELY FOR THE "KEEPERS"

> **Instructions for Required Action Steps**
> - **Discuss:** How can we keep behavioral feedback simple but make it meaningful?
> - **Determine:** How often should behaviors be reported?
> - **Consider:** Should behaviors be on the same report card as academic grades? Should the behavior reporting tool be a chart, checklist, or spreadsheet via digital or paper means?

Strategy: Think about how you have given feedback to improve non-academic behaviors throughout your career as an educator. If you are new, how were you given feedback in your K-12 experience? Then consider the effectiveness of the feedback. Did it elicit action on the part of the student to improve? Meaningful feedback must be actionable.

Next, think about a reasonable number of reporting times for these behaviors. Could it be as simple as the end of a marking period? Is that often enough? There is no *right* answer here. You will have to choose what is best for your students and yourself.

Strategy (student involvement): Take all of the student suggestions from Challenge Two and verbally share each one. Do students have ideas on layout and design for behavioral feedback? Absolutely! They are also a gold mine of insight to determine which behaviors are important not only in the classroom but also in their daily lives.

Students are so tech savvy that they may surprise you with a simple yet meaningful reporting tool.

What is the best way to give feedback on behavior without it being just another thing added to your teacher plate? If it is a burden to the teacher, then it could actually cause more headaches than productivity. How can we keep it simple but make it meaningful? When will non-academic behaviors be reported? What kind of reporting scale is best?

Meaningful feedback must garner action from the student. If there is misbehavior, simply identifying it will not change anything. After a quick identification (which the student can do as easily as the teacher), focus on the solution. Talk with the student about what an appropriate choice would be, and set a goal together for improvement. Again, never forget your power as a role model in the classroom. Students will observe and take in everything you do, so model the behavior you expect from your students!

The most powerful means of feedback is a personal conversation. Announcing misbehavior to the entire class does not support growth in individual students and is not effective feedback. A quick dialogue with a student to pinpoint their specific behavior and determine a path to improve it provides not only clarity for the student but also the ability to chart a course forward.

We don't have to track non-academic data for everyone every day. Collect data on a consistent but manageable basis. Look for trends over time. Don't let one student having an exceptionally rough day skew your data. We are human, and we all have bad days from time to time. Recognizing that a one-time incident is *just that* will ensure that sporadic instances of poor behavior don't misrepresent the trends throughout the marking period. Data collection on behaviors is just as important as gathering evidence of learning if we are going to give it weight on a report.

Non-academic behavioral reports can be delivered to parents in a variety of ways. A place for them on the report card sends a powerful message of the importance placed on behaviors. The information can also be delivered by a separate checklist or spreadsheet that accompanies the academic report card. No matter what delivery method is used, make sure the information gets directly to the parents involved! Know your community—would it be more beneficial to send reports digitally or through the mail? Keep in mind that this reporting is just one piece of communication. Emailing or calling parents to let them know about their student's behavior (positive or negative) opens an essential conversation and includes them in the support system for their child.

Challenge Three should provide you a platform to give effective, meaningful feedback for non-academic behaviors. This feedback should drive students to *own the process* and strengthen their skills which will support their academic achievement. Behaviors and academics go hand in hand to develop successful students, but communication of them should remain separate for accuracy in reporting.

Reflect:

_____

_____

_____

_____

_____

_____

"Education is the key to success in life, and teachers make a lasting impact in the lives of their students."
                                            -Solomon Ortiz

Together, teachers and students can discuss positive behaviors and their powerful impact on learning. Through this process, students know that they are responsible for their actions and that the teacher is on their side working with them to grow and improve. Holding students accountable for behaviors does not mean including them in the grade but **does mean** setting clear expectations and following through with conversations and goal setting. Parents and students are much more receptive to behavior feedback when it does not reduce the academic grade.

Another activity that significantly impacted the behaviors in my classroom was to mutually establish norms. This was done as a "circling the wagons" exercise where we came together as a class and brainstormed expectations not only for the students but also for me as the instructor. Once we got a manageable list in student-friendly language, we put up the question, "Are all these items things you can live with and expect yourself to follow?" Once the norms were agreed upon, it was our joint commitment to hold ourselves and each other accountable. By cleansing the behaviors from the grade and cleaning them up with clear goals and expectations, we created a shared ownership of the classroom culture.

One of the classroom norms that came up consistently was appropriate use of technology. In my classroom, we had a BYOD (Bring Your Own Device) policy, so I had a variety of devices show up to class each day. Students brought everything from smartphones, to tablets, to laptop computers.

There was one class that simply referred to their norms by a number. When the students had written and collectively decided on them, they assigned a number to each. They felt that this would be easier for accountability purposes. During one of my classes early in the process, I heard two students interacting. "Number four," I heard one student say to another at his table. There was no reaction from the other student. "Number four," the student insisted. He nudged his classmate and nodded over toward the agreed upon list of norms. Using technology appropriately was number four on the list. The student was playing a game on his phone rather than using it for educational purposes, and his classmate was holding him accountable. At that moment, I knew we were on the right path. Everyone shared the responsibility for creating an environment conducive to learning. We were practicing accountability without grading it, all the while building a strong, positive culture.

Let's face it. Academics and behaviors are tied to one another and always have been. In fact, integrating academic support and behavior support systems have proven to be extremely successful. An article from the RTI Action Network called, "Integrating Academic and Behavior Supports Within an RTI Framework," states, "Providing behavior supports may be effective in improving academic outcomes, and providing academic supports is related to improved social behavior functioning." When a student has consistent problems with timeliness and work quality, the academic achievement suffers. When these two things are pictured side by side, the connection is crystal clear. Behaviors are the processes by which we learn. This is not to say that there is always a perfect correlation. On occasion, there is a mismatch. A student can have poor work habits, but be highly successful with proficiency of the standards. Another may exhibit positive behaviors yet struggle academically. Those two situations should provoke thought and reflection for you as a teacher. What is fueling the mismatch? Does Maria need more challenging, complex work? Is the work at a level that no matter what Jacob does, he cannot find success? The beauty is that the separation of academic achievement from behaviors not only cleanses our grades but also provides invaluable information to move our students forward in both areas.

As you begin to observe and document academic achievement and behaviors separately, can you expect to see an improvement in student motivation? Absolutely! Research indicates that when we move closer to achieving a goal, it triggers a part of the brain linked to motivation. (Csikszentmihalyi, 1997). Thinking of this as a "quick fix" will only lead to stress. The grade cleanse will be refreshing as long as you keep reminding yourself to take baby steps, slow down, and celebrate every small victory. Keep it simple!

Taking our Grading Cleanse is a bold move. Do not underestimate the power of the status quo.

"Change is never easy. Roughly 70 percent of change efforts fail or are derailed."
   - <u>Who Killed Change?</u> by Ken Blanchard and John Britt

Middle School Students Self-Assess Behaviors

Katie Budrow, a sixth grade science teacher at Caruso Middle School in Deerfield, Illinois, says, "When I started having students self-report about behaviors, my biggest concern was that they would inflate their ratings. What I found was that inflated ratings were few in number, and I was able to easily cite specific evidence about why I disagreed with their assessment. The majority of the time, the students are *spot on* in self-assessing their behavior."

Here is what it looks like/feels like in her classroom:

In my science classroom, I put a lot of emphasis on both academics and behavior. However, we make sure to talk about them separately. Both have a lot of importance, and addressing them separately makes them both significant and more meaningful.

For behaviors, students report on four separate categories on an online form:

1. Perseverance
2. Pride in your work
3. Self-directedness
4. Respect

They report how frequently they exhibit each behavior. For each category, they choose among the following levels:

- Almost all of the time
- Most of the time
- Some of the time

The questions they answer are as follows:

- **Perseverance:** How often do you show perseverance or grit? Do you give up when things get hard or do you push through?

- **Pride in your work:** How often do you show pride in your work? Is it of a high quality and done on time?

- **Self-directedness:** How often do you do exactly what is expected of you without anyone telling you to do so? Are you a self-directed learner in the science classroom?

- **Respect:** How often do you show respect? Do you respect peers, adults, and property?

- **Reflect on your overall behavior in class:** What are your areas of strength? What are some things you can improve?

But I don't have time for this!

If you are thinking this will take up too much time, remember that the students fill out a very simple form online for me to review/analyze. I take their self-analysis and see if I agree with their assessment. **The majority of the time, the students are** *spot on.* If I agree, their comments are reported to their parents. If not, I'll make changes, discuss with parents, and have a personal conversation with the student about why.

Great conversations come out of the open-ended reflection question as well. I've had students give insight on learning styles, seating preferences, self-pacing, and creativity. This feedback is essential to coaching student success. Seeing students become intrinsically motivated to improve in each category is exciting.

In individual conversations, we break down the definition of the targeted behavior, and I then ask the student questions about what that behavior looks like and how we can achieve it. The personal conversations dig down into the *why*, and we create action steps to move forward. **The amount of behavioral growth that comes out of these conversations is phenomenal.**

While the benefits to having students self-assess are many, the one that stands out to me is the **new level of student ownership** for the classroom. Now that I have an effective way to report student behavior, academic grades have become a much better reflection of student learning.

CLEANSE NUMBER TWO

CAN I SHIFT THE LANGUAGE FROM
GRADE FOCUSED TO LEARNING FOCUSED?

"Grades are not compensation (you do that, I'll give you this). They are communication. Change the metaphor, and the paradigm shifts."
-Rick Wormeli

Do you want your students "fixated" on grades or learning?

As sometimes happens on a typical day in my classroom, "the line" had formed. All teachers know what this is—you are moving about the classroom supporting kids, giving feedback, and assessing work. Then, all of a sudden, you have a trail of students following behind you like you are a mother duck. So, once I had a free moment (or decided that I needed to attend to the line before it got any longer), I paused and started assisting the first student in line. This student was partially done with a piece of work and wanted me to take a look. As I started to read what he had written, I overheard the conversation that was happening between the students who were second and third in line. "I'm going to ask her what grade she would give this," said the second student in line, pointing to a writing draft in his hand. To give a little background, I did not grade formative work in my classroom. I gave the students actionable feedback and only assigned a proficiency level to summative work. This was a *draft*—definitely formative work. "Dude, she isn't gonna talk to you about grades," explained the third student in line. "You'd better figure out a way to talk about learning, or she isn't going to talk to you." This student had shifted his focus from grades to learning.

This shift would have been impossible if I didn't change the language I used with my students first. The change was not easy, because even though I had a strong desire to move the culture of my classroom to one of learning, the language of grading and compliance had become an ingrained habit. Cleansing my language took a lot of thought, reflection, and analysis. I had to think about the words I used, like *points* and *earn*, and shift them to *proficiency levels* and *demonstrate*. I had to think about how I introduced assignments and assessments—the status quo is to talk about what is required for a certain grade rather than what the students will be learning. Opening the discussion about a new unit, assignment, or assessment with the **learning targets** established the main purpose as *learning the standard*. Leading with language that gets students thinking about the minimum they have to do for a grade works against the desire to center the classroom or school on learning.

"What did you learn today?" is a routine question all parents, teachers, and relatives ask kindergarten students. However, around third or fourth grade, adult language changes to, "What did you make on that test?," "How are your grades?," and "Did you make honor roll?" Primary grade teachers have it right, and then we steer students away from the main reason they attend school—to learn. Establishing consistent language that hooks students on learning has nothing to do with receiving a grant, improving your school building, the clientele you serve, or any other factors outside of your control.

Think about it. Does a student with poor grades know he needs to bring them up? Of course! Then how does it make him feel when you tell him he needs to bring up his grades? Do you tell an overweight person that he needs to lose weight or a smoker that he needs to stop smoking? These are socially inappropriate comments that provoke anger and damage relationships. Identifying the problem will not help solve the problem. Your daily language will either build up or tear down your rapport with students.

Cleanse Two challenges you to listen to what you say, how you respond to questions, and what your students are hearing from you routinely. Do they hear you pulling for them? Do they hear that their primary purpose is *grades*—or *learning*? This is an opportunity to develop, replace, and consistently use a language of learning. Expect a natural improvement in teaching habits, more student engagement, and a noticeable increase in student success.

CHALLENGE ONE

REFLECT ON YOUR DAILY LANGUAGE
DOES IT CENTER AROUND LEARNING OR GRADING?

Instructions for Required Action Steps

- **Gather:** Consider the language (words, phrases) you most commonly use in your classroom.

- **Analyze:** What does the language you use communicate to your students?

- **Reflect:** Are there some changes that can be made through language to shift the focus from a grade to learning?

Strategy: Once again, use sticky notes to gather words and phrases that are routinely used with students throughout the day and that are related to their assignments, work, grades, etc. Analyze each sticky note individually, and determine if the word or phrase emphasizes the importance of doing their work, earning grades, or learning? Separate the sticky notes that only emphasize learning. What are the students hearing? Do students hear more language about doing their work, earning grades, or learning?

Strategy (student involvement): Students are great at holding teachers accountable for their change in language. Ask them to *call you out* on what you say if you shift back to talking about compliance or grading. This can be fun for students and will help you make sure your language is cleansed. Having the students identify them will also help *them* change their language so that everyone is on the same page and using common language.

With all of the pressure on teachers to have high achievement on test scores, emphasizing the state testing over learning can become easy. When a teacher declares, "This will be on your achievement test," this implies that the goal is having high test scores, and learning fades into the background. How much academic time is spent on teaching students how to take the state test?

Many teachers believe their main purpose is to prepare their students for middle school, high school, college, or whatever next level. "I am just trying to prepare you for high school," however, does not affirm that learning is our top priority.

Watch what you say! Use wisdom and discernment in your daily language with students. Our words matter. If we wonder why kids are so concerned about grades, all we have to do is reflect on their classroom experience. Let's soak our students in words that define our purpose.

Learning motivates and has no end. Remember, the purpose in shifting our language is about one thing—student success. The language used in a school system or classroom cannot be completely transformed in a matter of a few months, but the framework to continually support that change is attainable. **When students hear harmony in language from the adult staff every single day, learning will become a healthy, long-term intrinsic motivator for students.**

Challenge One should get you thinking about the language that drives your classroom culture. The action steps provide a framework for reflection and analysis to improve communication and conversations between you and your students as well as improve how the kids talk with one another.

Reflect:

_____

_____

_____

_____

_____

_____

CHALLENGE TWO

CREATE A CULTURE FOR LEARNING BY ELIMINATING NON-ESSENTIAL LANGUAGE AND REPLACING IT WITH HEALTHY TERMINOLOGY

Instructions for Required Action Steps

- **Analyze:** Evaluate both lists from Challenge One.

- **Decide:** Choose language to be eliminated in your classroom or school.

- **Determine:** Agree on learning-centered words and phrases.

- **Write:** Create a purpose statement that clearly defines words and phrases to guide all communication regarding grading.

Strategy: Ask yourself—"If I am committed to emphasizing grades as a reflection of learning, then what words and phrases must be drastically reduced or changed in my daily language?"

Discuss with colleagues the language used in your school and classrooms that will soak the students in a learning-centered school culture. Once that language is established, sharing with students the clear purpose for grading will be easy.

Strategy (student involvement): Students can help figure out how to replace some of the compliance and grading language in the classroom. Having them brainstorm some of the new language to be used will not only get them thinking about it but will also help them to start using it!

Classic questions from students:

"Are you going to grade this?"

"How much will this count?"

"How many points off is it for _____ (insert a requirement)?"

Even our top students consistently ask these questions, and it drives us crazy. They ask because they are trying to determine two things:

1. "Am I going to do the assignment?"
2. "If I decide to do it, how much effort will I give?"

When these questions are asked, we need to hit the *pause* button. Is this conversation going to be about the worth of an assignment being associated with points and grades, or is it going to be about learning? This has happened time and time again in classrooms without a second thought. This discussion was commonplace for my students and me for years. We need to take the time to change our approach so that students will consistently hear the true purpose of our assignments.

The traditional response is, "Yes, this will be graded and worth __ points." And since the question is irritating, teachers may even have a knee jerk reaction and say something like, "I may even double the points because I have told you over and over to stop asking that question!" A *cleansed* teacher uses this question as an opportunity to redirect student thinking and say something like this: "Everything we do is important. This assignment/assessment will help us see what you have learned so far so that we can plan next steps."

There are many other healthy responses to these "classic" questions, such as, "Have you learned this standard?" or "Can you show me the learning?" Throughout our grading cleanse, teachers will become extremely sensitive to these types of questions and use them to redirect.

Everything we do in our classrooms is communication, from the words we use during instruction to the information we give our students about an assignment or assessment. The language must shift not only verbally but also in written form. Instructions for assignments have to be focused on the learning outcomes. Formative assessments must be focused on feedback to move forward rather than some kind of judgement in the form of a grade. Even summative assessments can be framed or transformed to ensure continual movement forward for learners instead of being centered on judgment and an end to learning.

Changing the *words* we use as educators is difficult. Cleansing our language must happen if we want students to stop thinking about how much things are worth and start focusing on learning. Students are not "earning" in the classroom. They are acquiring knowledge, practicing skills, and developing understanding that will take them forward.

Do you want your students to be obsessed with grades or learning? Synonyms for the word *obsessed* include: engrossed, absorbed, fanatical, and hooked. Many of our best students have become so "fanatical" about their GPA, that learning has taken a backseat to being in the top ten percent or becoming valedictorian.

Many steer clear of courses they really need and take classes with the reputation of being an *easy* "A". Other students learn how to *figure out* their teachers, earn enough points to pass, and are never motivated to do their best. When students are "hooked" on grades and points, then school turns into a game rather than a place to learn.

One of the best ways to reduce the number of students playing the "points game," is to replace conversations about what the grading outcome will be with what the learning outcome will be. This shift took time for me—I had spent ten years of my teaching career talking about points, percentages, grades, what students had to do to get a certain grade, and the list goes on. With practice and an active focus on what I was saying to my students, I was successful in making the change. From time to time, I would still catch myself talking about a grade with a student rather than their learning, and I would have to stop myself. Eventually, I got better and so did the kids. The example from earlier in this chapter highlights the change in language that happened: "Dude, she isn't gonna talk to you about grades. You had better figure out a way to talk about learning, or she isn't gonna talk to you." The kids got so good that they would *call me out* on my language if I made a mistake!

Let's be clear. We are not adding **healthy learning language** to your daily plate. If you try adding new terminology to what you are already doing, then you may feel "buried alive." Hoarding is the compulsion to accumulate and store large quantities of nonessentials. Hoarders cannot throw anything away. A popular television show, "Hoarders-Buried Alive," tells stories of hoarders struggling with behavior that has made everyday existence unbearable for both themselves and their loved ones. Adding healthy learning language without eliminating inappropriate words and phrases will be counterproductive. Let go!

Here are a few examples to consider:

- Trade "Points" for "Levels of Learning"
- Trade "Scores" for "Evidence"
- Trade "Zero" for "Lack of Evidence"

Language is critical. All of us react negatively to certain terms and respond positively to others. Would you rather be on a "diet" that restricts what you can eat or "cleanse" your body of toxins? The word *responsibility* might be the main culprit in shifting the focus off of learning. At the beginning of one of my presentations to a large high school staff recently, I asked for a show of hands if they agreed with this statement: "Our main job is to teach our students responsibility." Every hand went up without hesitation. The room became very quiet after my follow-up question, "How many of you are highly qualified to teach responsibility?"

The emphasis on *responsibility* generates statements like, "If you do your work and bring up your grades, then you will pass." This is improper language in a culture of learning. Students hear that doing their work is more important than learning. They get the message that school is about making good grades, and if you happen to learn something—that is also okay.

Requiring a certain number of grades per week or marking period is detrimental to student learning. This can force teachers to put formative work in the grade book that "counts" when students are just embarking on their journey with learning targets and standards.

Do you use language that is purposeful and well-designed or dysfunctional and confusing? How would you describe the language in which you marinate your students on a daily basis? How would you change the language in your classroom to ensure that students are focused on learning instead of earning grades?

Challenge Two should support a change in language and provide examples of how to make that change. Don't forget that a change in language is not easy. The first step is to choose what words will replace those that move your focus away from learning. After that, consistent awareness and practice will make the shift permanent.

Reflect:

_____

_____

_____

_____

_____

_____

"Children do not choose to come to school. They have to. They come to school to learn, not compete for marks."

— <u>Learning About Learning</u>, Nov. 2013

A window into the classroom of Jason Ozbolt, an educator at Lockport Township High School in Lockport, Illinois

Students in my World History class were working on the causes of World War I leading to the start of the war. One student in particular, John, was having a hard time understanding the details and examples of the major causes. I sat down by the desk for a few minutes, and we were talking about supplemental resources that he could look at to help. Suddenly a fellow classmate, Tim, who overheard our conversation, got up and approached us. My first reaction was that Tim had a question and could not wait until I was done, but then he chimed in with, "John, if you are having a hard time, I can help you. I already know that standard." I looked at John, and he nodded his head in agreement. He got up, collected his things, and took a seat next to Tim. The two sat together, and I observed them for the remaining ten minutes of my class. They talked about each cause and the examples that went with them, working through the misconceptions and John's difficulties. Tim shared his notes and the resources he had collected in his learning and freely used them to help John understand and grow his knowledge. As far as I knew, Tim and John were not good friends outside of class, simply classmates. Seeing that the culture fostered in my classroom was one of collaboration and compassion and not competition was refreshing.

For years, the question was, "How many points for an 'A'?" or "How much is this worth?" For years, my language emphasized points and completion rather than content information and student learning. There needed to be a change in my classroom, as I could not go on like this forever. This was driving me crazy. Then it hit me. If I wanted my students to change, then I needed to change my language and approach. As I analyzed my language, I realized why students were fixated on grades while learning had taken a back seat.

I realized immediately how uncomfortable and difficult it is to change, but I was totally committed. With patience and persistence, the students followed suit, and my classroom culture changed for the better. Students were talking in the language of learning. Each student wanted to know where they were in their journey and what they needed to do to improve. The conversations I had with students were of a collaborative nature: "What can I help you improve on?" and "What do you think your next steps are?"

Student language changed as well: "I need to probably study more before I assess." and "We need to work better as a group and re-check our work." Top students who had previously kept their learned secrets of success to themselves began sharing with others because competition had faded away. I was shocked at how quickly my underachieving students started to feel safe and motivated. After the switch, failure was not an option for students. "I can't" were not words used unless they were followed by the word "yet." Students felt supported and, in turn, their confidence was built so they would take risks. And when they failed, and they did, they were more resilient and bounced back to continue to grow and learn. Students were liberated to achieve to the best of their ability and feel supported along the way.

As a teacher, I think you have to ask yourself this question: "Do you want your students fixated on grades or learning?" Persistence on my part was necessary to keep the focus on the learning. The majority of a student's day is in a classroom of *points* and *percentages*. So keeping the philosophy alive and the focus on learning was a daily commitment. Changing my classroom culture rekindled my passion for teaching and strengthened my rapport with students, as it centered on not only their learning but also on their development as an individual. Students knew without a doubt that I cared not just for their learning in my class but for their growth as individuals. My students were also empowered to become advocates for their own learning, and in turn, my students learned to advocate for themselves and for their needs independently. The change was worth it, and I will never go back!

"There are two primary choices in life: to accept conditions as they exist or accept the responsibility for changing them."

-Denis Waitley

Shifts in language will have a huge impact on classroom culture. Cleanse Two will lead to significant changes for teachers and students and is a natural second step in the process.

Language is very powerful. Framing all conversations around *learning* guides students to understand that learning is valued over grades. Proficiency levels and grades are communication rather than something that is earned or given by the teacher. We cannot expect changes in how our students communicate unless we change our language first. Kids are very used to assigning value to grades over learning, and our challenge is to turn that around.

PART TWO

PUTTING STANDARDS & LEARNING TARGETS IN STUDENT FRIENDLY LANGUAGE AND DETERMINING CLEAR PROFICIENCY LEVELS

"Students can hit any target they can see and will hold still for them."
-Rick Stiggins

Two of my best teachers were chosen by the state department to spend eighteen months writing an online curriculum for sixth, seventh, and eighth grade math. This became a learning experience for all of us. The only space available for them to work each day was in my conference room which was right next to my office. I was excited at first because this work would provide a valuable, hands-on resource for all our students in one of their most difficult subjects. The conference room was converted to a work area with state-of-the-art technology and workstations. When these two exceptional math teachers decided to start with separating and clarifying the learning targets, they began by listing each standard by grade level on white boards. I visited daily just to watch, listen, and learn. I noticed after a couple of months that they were putting a line through each standard once completed. I asked both teachers, "So now that you have gotten into a groove, what is the toughest part of writing the online math curriculum?" Both teachers rolled their eyes and started laughing. "When we start a new standard," they explained, "using the language given to us by the state, it takes us at least one whole day, sometimes two, to figure out what the learning targets are exactly.

We use a dictionary, thesaurus, Google search, etc. and sometimes end up arguing over what specifically should be taught."

These excellent math teachers had to study, argue, and analyze for at least a day in order to clarify the learning targets because the language was not in student-friendly form. After presenting to nearly a million teachers in twenty-one states, I can count on every teacher roaring with laughter when I ask this question: "Why does your state send you student academic standards that are written in language similar to the King James version of the Bible?" This hits a nerve in every school, in every state, at every grade level. An important part of our grade cleanse is to create clear learning targets that are in student-friendly language.

After cleansing behaviors out of grading and making the shift to learning-centered language, the next step is to make sure that the standards, learning targets, and proficiency levels are *crystal clear*. This ensures transparency in grading. Part Two of **Grade Cleanse** digs into what happens when teachers and students are on the same page with their expectations for learning. Cleansing the language of the standards (Cleanse Three) and establishing clear proficiency levels (Cleanse Four) are natural next steps to improving the accuracy of grading practices.

Teachers are handed a large number of standards from the state or national level and are charged to teach them with fidelity. However, if they are simply posted in classrooms without any further action, they become nothing more than *wallpaper*. We have seen many teachers do just this. Why? There are many schools that require teachers to post the standards. They get hung up at the beginning of the year or the start of each unit, and the box is checked-off for the teacher when an evaluator or administrator comes in to do a walk-through.

Another reason standards get left in the *background* is *understanding*. Most state standards are worded in ways that are difficult for educators to decipher, let alone for students and parents to understand. Emphasis is not placed on teachers sitting down and talking about what the standards really mean. A good amount of time is needed to break things down and delve into the complexity of the standards, but the time is well worth it! This was realized by the exemplary math teachers from my school. With so many demanding tasks, you might be thinking: "Where will I find the time?" We have to remember — when time is taken to truly understand the standards, we save time in the long-run. We save time with our students, because guiding them through the process of *understanding* becomes easier. We save time writing curriculum, because the end goals are clear. We save time grading, because we have a straightforward idea of the evidence that will show mastery of the standards. Effective writers don't try to impress readers by using uncommon or *showy* words. They use *familiar* words to keep readers engaged. Most state standards include language that is full of *educational jargon*. This language needs to be broken down to support students and parents alike.

There is a pitfall to avoid when dealing with the standards and learning targets. Once the standards are analyzed and broken down into targets the first time, the work can be seen as "done" and not revisited for some time. Don't let this happen. The conversations about standards and learning targets need to happen fluidly every year. The more we teach our standards, the more we understand them. The more we dialogue with our colleagues and share the learning, the more our growth impacts student learning. These are living and breathing documents, so continue to edit to ensure clear language that is easy for your students to grasp. Keep in mind that we must remove all non-essential practices from our teacher plate and work smarter, not harder.

CLEANSE NUMBER THREE

CAN I CREATE CLEAR LEARNING TARGETS
THAT ARE IN STUDENT FRIENDLY LANGUAGE?

The simplest analogy to hold on to while moving through Cleanse Three is a response to this question which was posted during an online, standards-based learning chat (#sblchat): "Why is it important to have clearly communicated learning targets?" Embrace this golf analogy: "Not having clearly communicated learning targets is like standing on the first tee and not knowing where the hole is. You might find it someday after a lot of wasted time and frustration."

Years ago, discussions with students about learning targets and objectives were very different than they are today. I am a little embarrassed to admit that as a student, I never thought of school in terms of what I needed to know, understand, or be able to do. Rather, I saw the objectives as completing assignments, taking notes, and taking assessments. The mindset was *task* before *learning* rather than *learning* before *task*. I came into class each day focused on the activities I would be expected to complete as well as any homework that was to be assigned. Maybe I saw the objective as the class title—mathematics, science, and so on. I was supposed to learn math. I was supposed to learn science. I assumed if I completed my assignments, then I would learn what I was supposed to learn. However, what I was specifically supposed to walk out of class knowing was not the focus for me or my teachers. Objectives existed, but they were not communicated as more important than the *tasks* we were to accomplish as students. "I teach it, and it is the student's responsibility to get it," was the time-honored classroom model. As a beginning teacher, I took the same approach: "I taught it. They should know it." I now see the fault in this. Clearly communicating the learning targets never crossed my mind. Using the golf analogy, I assumed they knew where the *hole* (target) was, but upon reflection, I am pretty sure they didn't know as often as I thought.

CHALLENGE ONE

DETERMINE THE STANDARDS FOR LEARNING

Instructions for Required Action Steps

- **Find:** Compile the national/state/locally developed standards for each content area or course that you teach.

- **Write:** Break each standard down into smaller learning targets, and write these learning targets in student-friendly language.

- **Read and Revise:** Read them again, and read them again! Revise.

Strategy: In small groups of teachers (with a variety of grade levels or content areas), pull out a standard. Have a teacher who teaches outside of your grade level or content area look at that standard. Let them break it down into language that makes sense to them. Having someone outside your realm look at it is important. If the reworked language makes sense to *them*, it will work for students and parents.

Standards are everywhere in this educational age. Common Core State Standards, Next Generation Science Standards, College, Career, and Civic Life Standards, the list goes on and on. Most educators are handed their state or national standards, and often there are so many, teachers feel overwhelmed from the start. Cleanse Three will help you clearly define your standards to make them useful and valuable tools in your classroom. **And remember, if you start to feel overwhelmed, slow down and take a baby step forward.** Instead of trying to do all of the standards, pick a few, and get used to the breaking-down process first.

Coaches, choir directors, and band directors are experts at simplifying language for very complicated learning targets. In discussing this with a large middle school and high school staff recently, I called on the head football coach to give an example. He immediately stood up and gave this excellent illustration: "On our team, when our defense intercepts a pass, every player and coach screams the word 'Oskee' so the players on the field know within a second or two to reverse their course because our team now has the football. Everyone knows what it means and what to do. I can only imagine what language the state would use to confuse and complicate what we have simplified. It might sound like: The players must be able to recognize, analyze, and react to the transition required when reversing their main purpose from defending the opponents intentions to move the ball forward to blocking and properly advancing the football towards their goal line." Laughter filled the room, and everyone got the point.

A very successful softball coach stresses simple and consistent language with every player and coach. She said, "When I tell my athletes to 'push to three,' they all know this means to drive through the ball and finish. Consistency is key!" Just like coaches with their players, teachers and students must have learning targets in simple language they can understand.

Teachers are worried that if they don't put the exact words of the state standards up in their rooms, their evaluation may be affected. In truth, if the teacher will simply let the students know at the beginning of the lesson what they want them to walk out of the room with that day, reinforce those learning targets in the middle of the lesson, and wrap up the lesson by revisiting the learning targets, the teacher has done exactly what he or she was supposed to do that day. All students, when approached, should be able to tell anyone what the goal of the day is exactly. If they cannot, you have not put the learning targets in kid-friendly language and communicated them effectively with your students. Finally, taking time with colleagues to revisit and tweak learning targets each year is time well spent.

Challenge One should help you see your standards as a useful classroom tool rather than something that bogs you down as a teacher. The standards need some help to maximize their benefit, and this is where the work of the teacher to simplify the language is critical. The *messy tape* of jargon-laced standards becomes *clear targets* that guide students to success in their learning. Remember, "students can hit any target they can see and will hold still for them."

Reflect:

_____

_____

_____

_____

_____

_____

CHALLENGE TWO

FOCUSING SPECIFICALLY ON THE <u>VERBS</u> IN THE STANDARDS, DECIDE WHAT THEY MEAN WITH YOUR COLLEAGUES

Instructions for Required Action Steps

- **Find:** Highlight the verbs.

- **Discuss:** What do these verbs demand of you as a teacher?

- **Discuss:** What do these verbs demand of your students? How will they show evidence of learning?

Strategy: Take the standards selected for a given unit of study, and put each on a notecard. Hand all the standards out to the teachers on the team, and have them jot down one sentence indicating what the *verb* is asking the student to do. Circulate the cards until every team member has had a chance to examine the *verbs* for each standard, and offer at least one example of an appropriate assessment. Use these ideas as the foundation for a discussion on learning standards.

Building an understanding of the *learning standards* is a team effort. If individual teachers close their doors and develop their own meaning for standards, accuracy with grading does not improve. If I, as a teacher, have a different idea of what the standards mean than my counterpart across the hall, we will expect different evidence from students when it comes time to assess them. What's worse is that this practice turns teachers into *silos,* where doors get closed and teachers get possessive of what happens in their classrooms. They feel threatened when the time comes to talk about what they demand of their students, how they assess them, and how that leads to a determination of a grade. There is also the risk of parents wanting a certain teacher over another because of what they hear from other parents and older students who have come through the school. With a *cleanse* comes transparency which is essential for a strong and effective teaching team.

Take a sample seventh grade math standard from the Common Core State Standards:

> *7.NS.A.1 Apply and extend previous understandings of addition and subtraction to add and subtract rational numbers; represent addition and subtraction on a horizontal or vertical number line diagram.*

Following the action steps, we would first look at the verbs in this standard, which are *apply*, *extend*, *add*, *subtract*, and *represent*. This particular standard has quite a few verbs, so the discussion with colleagues about what they mean will not be quick. Verbs like *add* and *subtract* tend to have an easy-to-pinpoint meaning from teacher to teacher. *Apply*, *extend*, and *represent*, however, are very different. These are more complex verbs and are much more open to interpretation. Students need to *apply*, *extend*, and *represent* with their addition and subtraction to demonstrate mastery of the standard, and teachers talking about what that means is essential. Without discussion and collaboration, the meanings of these verbs can easily vary from classroom to classroom in terms of what we expect from students.

At this point, the *question of all questions* comes back into play: How are we going to find the time to do this? To counter: What will happen if we don't find the time? Will our students' grades become clearer? Will our students be able to *hold* the standards?

Action steps two and three should be repeated often for the sake of learning. We continually know and understand more as time goes on, so why wouldn't this apply to our own knowledge surrounding the standards? This work is never *done* just like learning is never done for our students. Not only do we learn more about the standards by revisiting them, but we can also improve instruction and assessment to get a more accurate view of proficiency with each passing school year. When we *know* better, we *do* better. Looking at standards multiple times leads us to knowing better.

Tory Atwood, Science Department Chair, Stewarts Creek High School, Tennessee

My science team meets every summer as a group to look at our standards for the year and to try and put them in language the students (and teachers) understand. We use this agreed upon wording when we put standards in our gradebook, so there is no discrepancy. Some examples of student-friendly language changes are as follows:

1. "Demonstrate the effect of gravity on objects," is changed to, "What is the weight?"

2. "Conduct, analyze, and communicate the results of an experiment that demonstrates the relationship between pressure and volume of gas," becomes, "Understand Boyle's Law."

3. "Conduct, analyze, and communicate the results of an experiment that demonstrates the relationship between temperature and volume of a gas," is simplified to, "Understand Charles' Law."

Students like to see where they are successful and where they struggle. Seeing both *successes* and *struggles* allows students to realize that they are not defined by their first score, and they are motivated by the opportunities to improve. I use the same proficiency levels as my state plus **LOE** for **Lack of Evidence** when extra practice is mandated until they get to a level. I have linked the levels to a percentage value in my gradebook, since our district has not changed to standards-based reporting—which makes this a *hybrid. See the Appendix for conversion ideas.*

Challenge Two should provide a method to break down standards as a team to determine what they demand from your students. This should be used as a *wash, rinse, repeat* process where the standards are analyzed, taught, assessed, and then revisited to learn more about them.

Reflect:

_____

_____

_____

_____

_____

_____

CHALLENGE THREE

MIRROR THE DISCUSSION WITH YOUR STUDENTS

Instructions for Required Action Steps

- **Provide:** Provide the unedited standards to the students.

- **Point Out:** Point out that the starting point for their discussions is highlighting the *verbs* in the standards.

- **Discuss:** Give students ample opportunities for discussion.

- **Monitor:** Monitor the discussion and encourage analysis/synthesis of the standards.

Strategy (student involvement): Take those standards and turn them into a meaningful classroom activity. Let the **students** clarify what the standards mean and break them down. This is a critical thinking assignment at its best! Focus on the *verbs* and what they mean for student work and products. Ask the students what they will need along the way to achieve the target. Once you come to an agreement about the meaning of standards and student needs, wonderful things will happen. First, students will know the precise direction they are headed. Refer to the golf analogy again—they know where the hole is! Second, they will take ownership of their learning once it is clear. Breaking down standards with your students may use a little more time than you feel comfortable with in the beginning, but you will gain the time back in the end. This may feel like a slower start to the unit of study, but you will be at a fervent pace by the end. A big part of this *Grade Cleanse* is pushing past that uncomfortable feeling that arrives when asked to do something new.

One teacher shared that she will often start a unit by putting a standard on the board using the exact same *unfriendly* language given to her. After dividing her students into small groups and giving each student a thesaurus and dictionary, she charges them with, "Let's come up with a way to break down this standard and write it in language that we can understand." Students analyze, synthesize, argue, and discuss for at least one class period. Each group makes a short presentation explaining what they came up with, and then they vote. Several teachers at various grade levels have tried this, and the feedback is extremely positive: "I love hearing them discuss which words they like the best. All students get engaged at the very beginning of the unit because they have input." Exploring strategies like this will actually save time and allow you to become more of a facilitator of student learning.

Taking time for the students to get involved in simplifying their standards is probably one of the most difficult tasks for teachers, because they feel they have limited time to teach and are cautious about wasting precious time at the beginning of a unit. Getting the students involved, however, will once again spend a little time to save quite a bit more. After state testing, there is often extra time that would be ideal for this. Have the students who are in the current class, who have already been through the course and know what is expected, rewrite the standards for next year.

Discovering strategies like this will saturate your students in higher-order thinking. When considering what is involved in higher-order thinking, *analysis* and *synthesis* are two verbs that commonly come up. *Analysis* involves the breaking down of what you read into its component parts in order to make it clear and understandable. *Synthesis* is the ability to "put together" the parts analyzed to create something *original.* Having students analyze the language of the standards your state has decided they are to learn and then create wording that makes sense to them is excellent practice for learning.

Challenge Three should give you the confidence to turn some of the decisions made in the classroom over to the students. They may surprise you with their ability to analyze standards, fully understand their meanings, and take ownership of their own learning!

Reflect:

_____

_____

_____

_____

_____

_____

CHALLENGE FOUR

PLACE THE LEARNING STANDARDS INTO A NATURAL PROGRESSION

Instructions for Required Action Steps

- **Analyze:** With colleagues, analyze and break down the standards into smaller pieces or skills to lay out a natural progression to mastery.

- **Rework:** With students, rework and write the targets in student-friendly language.

Strategy: Write one of your standards on a large piece of butcher paper. With colleagues, talk about how students in the past have moved to proficiency with that particular standard. Write down the steps and skills that they have shown along the way. Once they have brainstormed, put those steps in a logical order of progression. This shows how the learning targets *build* so that students and teachers have a *path* for learning.

Strategy (student involvement): Another way to break down standards into targets is to involve your students. If you have a natural progression already determined, share it with your students. Have them talk about the steps, and see if they make sense. If there is any language that they can change to make the target clearer, take their suggestions! When they understand the language, they can hit the target with more frequency and accuracy.

While working with some fantastic educators from Minnesota who are actively changing their grading practices, one teacher had an epiphany. In the state of Minnesota, many of the standards are already broken down into targets (benchmarks) for the teachers. We were having a discussion about these benchmarks and how they can be scaffolded for students throughout instruction. She was looking at them and said to me, "The benchmarks form the framework for me! They naturally get more and more complex as you move through and to the standard as a whole." This small realization was so significant for her. Diving deeply into standards and benchmarks is important even if the state has written them for you! This story says it all. She thought that she would have to do much of this work on her own (and at times she did), but she realized that the already constructed benchmarks would turn into the scaffolded targets for her students. They were a natural progression that students could follow, develop proficiency with, and eventually find mastery with the standard as a whole.

The more you divide the standard up, seeing where the deficiencies are becomes easier. For example, understanding *speed, velocity,* and *acceleration* is a common high school science standard. Each one of these are huge topics. If you lump them all together, you will never know where the real struggle is. Is it with *speed? Velocity? Acceleration?* Is there an issue with the math involved or the vocabulary? Break the standard down, and you will be able to more easily assess and remediate if need be.

If you used the suggestion from Challenge Three and had last year's class simplify the standards after state testing, their results can be analyzed and edited by the current year. This can be part of the "after assessment" activity. Typically, teachers spend time reteaching, and some students need to restudy and retake tests, so this would be an ideal time for available students to edit the wording of the standards. **The thing to remember is that you want all students to understand the standards at some point, and learning is not a race.** You do not want educational *bulimia* where students gorge themselves on the information and then regurgitate it on the test without really learning anything. Constantly reevaluating the wording of the standards with your students will help all involved stay engaged.

Keep in mind that you and your students will be constantly improving your understanding of the standards and ability to break them into targets, and this is both a joy and a challenge. In real estate, the golden rule is *location, location, location.* Think *simplify, simplify, simplify* so that students can *hold* the language of each standard. Dividing standards into meaningful pieces with a natural progression not only informs students of what they will need to do to show proficiency with the standards but also sparks student ownership. **Intrinsic motivation explodes when students are granted choice and control.**

Challenge Four should encourage you to create a scaffold or ladder for your learners to climb on their way to proficiency. This sets up a clear path for students and allows them to see where they are on the journey to proficiency. Knowing the checkpoints along the way allows for small, periodic celebrations on the way to success!

Reflect:

_____

_____

_____

_____

_____

Are the learning objectives of your classroom purposeful and well-designed or dysfunctional and confusing? Unclear or confusing words are a barrier to learning for many students. Just like a golf course is clearly laid out from tee to green, student success will dramatically improve when you establish clear learning targets in student-friendly language.

CLEANSE NUMBER FOUR

CAN I ESTABLISH CLEAR AND CONSISTENT PROFICIENCY LEVELS FOR ALL STAKEHOLDERS?

"It's time to abandon grading scales that distort the accuracy, objectivity, and reliability of students' grades. Percentage grading systems that attempt to identify 100 distinct levels of performance distort the precision, objectivity, and reliability of grades."

-Thomas R. Guskey

As a beginning teacher, the phrase "proficiency levels" was not anything that I connected with my grading practices. I didn't necessarily look at the depth or quality of the evidence my students produced let alone how it related to the standard or standards. With traditional tests and assignments, I counted the number of items right and wrong and allowed the computer to mathematically figure the grades from there. With writing samples, I used a rubric, but it did not effectively utilize proficiency levels. My rubrics counted the number of errors made, ensured that a specific word count was made, located all the vocabulary words and how they were used, etc. I didn't look at the *whole* product and how it communicated what was demanded in the prompt. I didn't check to see if the grammatical errors affected this communication or if they were small enough that the message wasn't lost. I'm certain that I never thought about why I used a percentage scale. My own teachers had used percentage scales when I was a student, so why should things be any different now? To take one assessment and come up with 101 different levels of proficiency (zero to one hundred) may very well be impossible, but the *status quo* had "worked" for a long time. Why would things need to change? What I failed to recognize is that differentiating among 101 levels is excruciatingly difficult when looking at student work. Algorithms don't equate to accuracy, and I needed to stop hiding behind the math in order to *own* my grading practices.

Since I wasn't using the language of learning (Cleanse Two), my students weren't either. They didn't look at their work and connect it to the standards and their level of proficiency. They would only see the *number right*, the *number wrong*, and the *percentage*. The only "levels" my students were familiar with were the 101 points of the percentage scale and their correlation with letter grades. This had nothing to do with the standards, and I wasn't helping the matter with the way I was talking to them about *learning*. This did not foster an environment of reflection, self-assessment, and action. Since the students were only looking at the points and grades on their assignments and assessments, they were missing a vital part of the learning process which includes analysis of their mistakes, reflection, feedback, and taking action to move learning forward. Once the grade was determined, that signaled a *stop* to the learning. From that point, the "old material" was not at the forefront of their thinking—it was time to move on to the next topic.

What would a cleaner system look like? A cleansed system reduces the number of levels in a significant way. Healthy grading uses meaningful levels that support learning. Many schools and teachers who have cleansed their practices use a four-level scale, which provides much more clarity.

More importantly, 101 levels eliminate the intrinsic motivation fueled by moving up from one level to the next. As mentioned, when a student receives a number grade on the 0-100 point scale, learning stops. Nobody is motivated to move up from an 81 to an 82, which makes the traditional grading scale useless as an effective way to motivate students and stimulate the learning process. Moving up on a four-level scale (that is focused on learning) feeds motivation. Think about the sense of accomplishment that a student feels when moving from a level two (basic understanding of a standard) to a level three (proficient with the standard) as opposed to moving from an 81 to an 82. This makes a huge difference!

Establishing clear proficiency levels, however, goes beyond changing from a percentage scale to a four-level scale. If we simply replace letters with numbers, we have done nothing to improve our practice and cleanse our grading methods. Cleanse Four demands that we consider the standard, learning targets, and student work that represent each level. It demands that we communicate this with students and parents so that they fully understand what is expected. It moves learning to the forefront.

Kids and parents understand the traditional system. Here's the status quo: Assignments and assessments are given, points are assigned, and grades are determined by how many points the students accumulate at the end of the marking period. This is the system most parents had when they were in school, and it was "good enough" for them. Parents may push back on a different scale in the beginning because it is not the way things have been done in the past. They may say things like, "The percentage scale is much more accurate than this new system," or "The math makes sense to me, but these levels do not." We can respond to the concerns with patience and clear communication. Change takes time, and a cleanse in grading practices is no different. Grading practices must be cleansed to increase student learning, and that's the *bottom line*. Once kids and parents know this to be true, letting go of the wide-ranging scale and replacing it with something more meaningful and practical becomes easier.

CHALLENGE ONE

DECIDE ON THE NUMBER OF PROFICIENCY LEVELS

Instructions for Required Action Steps

- **Identify:** Determine the number of proficiency levels currently in use.

- **Discuss:** Talk about the pros and cons of the current system.

- **Consider:** Discuss reducing the number of levels to less than six.

- **Determine:** Discern how many levels will work for your classroom, school, and/or district.

Strategy: In a group setting, ask teachers what the difference in learning is between a 72 and a 76 percent. This exercise points out the difficulty in defining levels of learning—let alone so many! Having a high number of proficiency levels also makes agreeing on what those levels mean in the collective group of teachers difficult. Discuss how a 101-level scale (0-100) is ineffective for communicating student proficiency and does not support teacher consensus with the various levels of student achievement.

Another item for discussion about percentage scales is the number of levels for a grade of *F*. Typically, 90-100 is an *A*, 80-89 is a *B*, 70-79 is a *C*, 60-69 is a *D*, and 59 and below is an *F*. This means that there are sixty different levels of failure. This section would be the most difficult for which to write descriptors! There simply aren't that many levels of failure when looking at student work. Consider the other end of the scale: Are there 11 different levels of *A* work? Deciding on how many levels of learning can be discerned helps teachers cleanse their grading with the healthy practice of limiting the number of proficiency levels.

Strategy (student involvement): Conduct the same activity, but this time involve the students. One idea would be to divide them into groups of three or four to think and discuss—starting with the number of proficiency levels. Even though experts recommend between two and six levels, letting students discuss before telling them is best. Then, have students discuss reasons why the experts might recommend a small number of levels. Student motivation and engagement increases significantly when they are allowed to have choices and control.

When determining the number of proficiency levels, experts recommend that *less is more*. Four is the most common number of levels. Teachers have a much easier time determining proficiency levels when there are clear descriptors tied to fewer levels. They can come together on what work meets the standard and what still needs some work. Students also have an easier time with fewer levels. Self-assessment becomes a more clear-cut endeavor if students don't have to decide whether their work is a 77 or 78, but instead, whether it is three (proficient) or a two (working toward standards). Having a lower number of levels truly increases accuracy in grading. When teachers and students alike have a clear idea of what each level means, they can better communicate what the grade means. Keeping in mind that baby steps energize us internally, you can expect student learning to *snowball* when they move up a level. Give yourself permission to reduce the levels of proficiency in your classroom, and the picture of learning becomes much more crisp for you and your students!

Challenge One should generate thought-provoking conversations and reflections. Taking the plunge and reducing proficiency levels will have a positive impact on your classroom and school culture when paired with the *language of learning*.

Reflect:

_____

_____

_____

_____

_____

_____

CHALLENGE TWO

WRITE DESCRIPTORS FOR THE PROFICIENCY LEVELS

Instructions for Required Action Steps

- **Brainstorm:** Consider a variety of descriptors for each of the proficiency levels.

- **Discuss:** Talk about the pros and cons of what each descriptor would mean for teachers and students.

- **Decide:** Determine which descriptors to use, and craft a plan to put them into place on a consistent basis in the classroom/school.

Strategy: Collaborative discussion among teachers and administrators can accomplish the task of crafting descriptors for each level of learning. Having both groups present for the dialogue will increase investment in the decisions made and support *all* in defending them to other staff, parents, students, and community members. Keep the descriptors short and concise so that everyone has a shared understanding of what they mean for student learning. The words that you choose matter, but the collective understanding of them matters more!

Are you working on cleansing your practices as an individual? Not to worry! This is the time to do some research and reach out to others in the field for examples. Then you can brainstorm and make some decisions about what will work for you and your students.

Strategy (student involvement): Have small student groups decide what they want to call each learning level. When turning things over to the students, *staying out of it* is very important. Otherwise, they will stop *thinking* and start trying to just please you. Let each group present their recommendations without making any final decision. After a healthy time for discussion, share the examples used in some schools, other classrooms, and any state descriptors that may exist. Then the decision can be made on the wording of the descriptors as a collective community of learners.

There are many ways to describe proficiency levels. As mentioned earlier, the importance lies on what you and your school determine as the meanings for those levels. The following is a short list of sample descriptors, but there are many others out there!

Examples of descriptors:

Level Four: *Distinguished, Advanced, Excellent, Excels*

Level Three: *Proficient, Meets Standards, Meets Expectations*

Level Two: *Developing, Working Toward Standards, Basic*

Level One: *Emergent, Does Not Meet standards, Below Basic*

Be aware that choosing the name for Level Four has been a significant topic of discussion by grading experts. For example, Thomas Guskey, Professor of Educational Psychology at the University of Kentucky, writes: "*Exceeds Standard* as the top level presents difficulties. If mastering a standard means hitting the target, then how can a student *exceed* hitting the target? An Olympic archer who places their arrow in the center of the bulls-eye has hit the target, not exceeded it. When a student hits the target, they have mastered the standard, not exceeded it." As you may have noticed, *exceeds* has been left off our previous list for this reason.

As a result of some experts' dislike for levels like *exceeds*, one state recently changed their four levels to: *Mastered, Approaching, On Track*, and *Below*. There is no consensus on four perfect names for the levels, so do your best, and use language that will be effective with *your* students and parents. Another idea is to use the term *Lack of Evidence (LOE)* to let students know they need more practice to "get on the board." Many teachers like this, especially at the secondary level, to encourage "extra practice." *Lack of evidence* simply communicates that the teacher will need more evidence to make a valid determination of a proficiency level. This encourages the student to produce evidence of learning, challenges the teacher to find that evidence, and intrinsic motivation is fueled. A very low grade on a percentage system can make success feel impossible for a student. What happens to motivation at this point? Let's tell students they can engage and achieve, and let's use grading practices that do the same.

A common question that arises from a discussion on proficiency levels is, "What is a four?" How do we determine when a student has somehow gone deeper with a standard and is able to prove it? When searching through the literature and reflecting on my own practice, there are a variety of answers to this question. As might be expected with the process of cleansing grading practices, there is no single, definitive answer. In *Understanding by Design*, Jay McTighe and Grant Wiggins discuss the highest level of proficiency with the word *transfer*. This is the ability of students to take their learning and apply it to new situations. One of the best ways to start a discussion on what level-four evidence looks like is to consider student exemplars. Teachers know who has gone *above and beyond* with a standard. Look at those work samples. What sets them apart from others that still show proficiency? What is different about them? Try this, and you just may find the answer to the *level four* question.

Challenge Two should foster candid conversations about student learning and what it looks like. In our experience, teachers feel as if they have been *let out of prison* with grading when they put four proficiency levels on the corner of their board and let go of the 101 point system. Transferring the conversation from *points* and *percentages* to *proficiency levels* gives way to a dialogue about learning rather than number crunching. The cleanse is on! We are all focused on one thing—learning!

Reflect:

_____

_____

_____

_____

_____

_____

CHALLENGE THREE

DECIDE HOW THE CHANGE WILL TAKE PLACE

WILL IT BE AT THE CLASSROOM, BUILDING, OR DISTRICT-WIDE LEVEL, OR WILL IT TAKE PLACE AS A PILOT PROGRAM?

HOW WILL THE PARENTS BE NOTIFIED?

Instructions for Required Action Steps

- **Determine**: Decide whether a pilot program will be implemented or whether the change will be school or district wide.

- **Look**: Review the process for cleansing grading practices, and make a plan for step-by-step communication with parents.

- **Communicate**: Get the word out to parents about the change process as soon as possible, starting with the paradigm shift.

- **Inform**: Keep parents informed at each stage of the transition in multiple ways.

Strategy: Research other districts who have cleansed their grading practices. Did they start with a pilot program or take it step by step with their school or district? What were their successes and challenges? You know your school and district better than anyone, and this decision must suit your needs and readiness to implement. After researching other districts, collaborate to decide about how to *scale* the cleanse. Are there a few teachers who are very enthusiastic and others that need to see some success stories to *buy in*? If so, a pilot program may be the perfect place to start. Is this something that, as a school or district, you feel passionate about and want to do as a systemic change? Whichever way you go, keep parents involved. Send written and digital communication home. Invite them in for parent nights as well as individual meetings to help them understand the process and get their questions answered.

Strategy (student involvement): Students can be the best advocates for a shift in grading practices, so get them involved in the parent communication piece. Once they have some success with the *cleansed* methods (and they will!), let them do some of the communicating. Happy kids = happy parents! When the language is consistent in the classroom and learning-focused, this is the language that is brought home by students. They will go home with positive attitudes and help bring the parents on board.

There are different ways to go about introducing and scaling healthier grading practices. Some districts form a pilot program with a few teachers who are enthusiastic about getting started and ready for a challenge. In this case, communication from the district/school to parents may not be very inclusive. There may be a general letter, email, or phone blast that mentions the pilot and where parents can go for more information. At this point, the communication falls heavily on the teacher with administrative support behind the scenes.

When I implemented healthier, *cleansed* grading practices in my classroom, it was not part of a school or district-wide change. I communicated early and often with my parents and encouraged questions. This is not an easy change for some, since *school* was not done this way when they were students, and it is not the *status quo*. I started with the *why* of the change and then explained how the process would look and what students would be producing. I talked about how behaviors are just as important as academics and that I would be reporting them separately. I talked about proficiency levels and why too many levels may not be the best way to communicate academic achievement.

When cleansing grading practices is going to be *scaled* for a school or district, communication becomes an "all hands on deck" undertaking. The topics remain the same, addressing the *why* for the change, how it will happen, and what will be produced. The message must be consistent from all parties, and the *language* comes into play yet again. When the language is inconsistent, parents will interpret the practices inconsistently, and the water is murky again.

Teachers need to explain why they are changing (even if this already appeared in information provided by administration). Parents need to be calmed and supported with any sort of change. Cleansing *practices* may make perfect sense to the educators involved, but bringing parents along is on a different level. Jargon that may make sense to teachers does not often make sense to parents or students. Bring the language of learning to the parents, and let them know you care. Don't leave parents in the dark! When something new is thrown to them without explanation, parents can feel sidelined and confused. Invite them to learn and become involved in the change process. Parents can become a beneficial asset and advocate for the *cleanse* and its impact on student learning.

Challenge Three should provoke thought on *scaling* the process of cleansing grading practices. Making well thought out, intentional choices about implementing and clearly communicating the plan is essential for success.

Reflect:

_____

_____

_____

_____

_____

_____

Is the water getting clearer? Are your grading practices becoming a more meaningful piece of communication for students and parents alike? *Grade Cleanse* is not a *quick-fix* approach to healthier grading practices—it is a bold but necessary change. This book offers a "move at your own pace" purification method that gives you time to *process* and *think*. Start small!

So far, you have done the following:

1. Separated behaviors from academic grades
2. Purified daily language to accentuate learning
3. Established clearly-defined/student-friendly learning targets
4. Formed learning levels that students can embrace and *own* their progress

Right now, student grades in your classroom are healthier, so stop and celebrate!

Your Classroom Culture is Your Choice

My daughter, Amy, is an excellent third grade teacher. On the first day of school, she establishes clear and consistent proficiency levels for her students and parents. She uses the same four learning levels as the state: *Mastered, Approaching, On Track,* and *Below Basic.* These four levels are not her chosen terminology, but she has settled on using the state language to help with consistency. Her students have data notebooks divided into each subject (math and science), broken down into each standard. Based on the most recent *evidence of learning,* the students record their learning level and review strengths and weaknesses for a few minutes each day. Instead of saying, "Bring up your grades," she soaks her students in the language of learning and encourages them to "move up a level." When a student moves up a level on any standard, she briefly celebrates with the entire class by playing the theme song, "Movin' On Up," from the classic television show, *The Jeffersons* (if you don't know it, just Google it!). Her students all dance for a moment because a classmate has improved his or her learning, which will result in an improved grade. Amy emphasizes *learning* over *grades*, and her parents and students love it. Her students are motivated long term because she has tapped into the fact that "when we move closer to achieving a goal, it triggers a part of the brain linked to motivation (Csikszentmihalyi, 1997)." The following letter from the parents of one of her students clearly reflects her total emphasis on learning.

Hi Amy,

To start this letter, I want to mention that third grade has been nothing short of amazing this year. As you know, Matt is our second child coming up through Gladeville Elementary, and although our experience with Gladeville has been absolutely incredible, our experience in your classroom has been the best thus far.

You have become a part of the Oldham family. While many kids blankly reply to the question "How was your day?" at the dinner table, we heard amazing story after amazing story of the neat things that Matt learned in your classroom. Matt brought home not only stories of "what he learned today," but also stories of your compassion, cleverness, fairness, and love for children. Kellie and I quietly listened to all of the good things that were happening in Matt's life as he detailed the "life of a third grader in Mrs. Wood's class." As I believe you spent a comparable amount of hours of the day with Matt as we did, we sincerely appreciate the strong moral and ethical values that you instilled in our son. He has become more confident in not only his academics but also with just being a fine young man.

The amount of effort you put into your classroom and the love of learning that you instill in your students is evident. Kellie returned from chaperoning several field trips impressed with your ability to control a large group of kids in a kind and patient manner. She repeatedly stated, "Amy sets the expectations for the children. The kids know what to expect and act accordingly." In fact, nothing made me feel better than coming to school on those occasional events and seeing you treat the kids with such dignity and respect. You gave the class your full attention, and each and every one of those children returned the favor because they knew what was expected of them. The genuine warmth you showed those children was amazing.

So what I would say is this. You have made a difference in the life of a child. You have been THAT teacher that impacts a child and makes a child's life better. In fact, you've made our whole family better. When Matt is 50, you'll be the teacher that he fondly remembers as the best teacher he ever had, and we are forever grateful for the impact that you've made on his life. You have taught him humility, patience, creativity, moral strength, and so much more.

A simple "thank you" cannot nearly begin to express our heartfelt gratitude, but thank you for everything you've done and all the effort you've put forth. You are, to put it simply, absolutely incredible! We'll deeply miss you next year.

Please enjoy a wonderful summer. You've earned it!

Re-read the letter:

1. How many times did the parent reference learning?
2. Can you find the term "grade" or "grades" mentioned?
3. Make a list of all the non-academic behaviors and traits the parent says their son learned from Amy.

Soak your students in the *language of learning*, knit the learning levels into your daily routine, and encourage every student to *move up*.

PART THREE

ALIGNING INSTRUCTION, PRACTICE, AND ASSESSMENT
PROVIDING CONSISTENT FEEDBACK TO MAXIMIZE STUDENT GROWTH

"Integrity is making sure that the things you say and the things you do are in alignment."

-Katrina Mayer

We have all heard the phrase, "Put your money where your mouth is." Not only is this applicable in everyday life, but it is also extremely important in classrooms and schools. When we state the standards and break them down into student-friendly learning targets, we had better "put our money where our mouth is" and align all daily instructional and assessment practices with the standards. When students ask, "Why are we doing this?" educators should pause and respond thoughtfully. Students should always know why they are doing something, and "because I said so" is not an acceptable answer. If learning targets are made clear but classroom experiences are not tightly aligned, then students will be lost and confused. The "gotcha" mentality will surface and trust will be sacrificed. To maximize learning, students knowing that every adult is pulling for them to succeed and not trying to "get them" is essential. There is no room for a "gotcha" approach in classrooms and schools. Once the targets are clear, our job is to directly align them with everything we do.

Feedback also falls within the parameters of being intentional and driven by the standards. To find their way forward, students need guidance from teachers in the form of effective feedback. Specific and timely feedback lets students know where they are and what steps to take next. The role of the teacher is not to publish information, but to facilitate learning. When teachers give effective feedback, students learn. However, the weight of delivering feedback does not solely fall on the teacher. Students can also learn to give and receive feedback from one another, which develops a culture of unity where all involved in the classroom (and school) are pulling for one another. An environment of *competition* is replaced by one of *collaboration*. Everyone is on the same team working for learning rather than trying to outscore others. Developing a routine for giving feedback will help share the responsibility and ownership among everyone in the learning community. Feedback is the cornerstone of learning. We can make feedback non-threatening and something students value in order to learn. Cleanses five and six take the learning targets and proficiency levels to the next step by putting them into action with alignment and feedback.

CLEANSE NUMBER FIVE
CAN I ALIGN EVERYTHING I DO IN MY CLASSROOM TO MY STANDARDS/LEARNING TARGETS?

Put yourself back in middle school with a project to complete for social studies class. The assignment is to learn about a region of the United States. You must create a poster which demonstrates your findings, including the importance of the region to the rest of the country. You do some research and place all the information and summarization of your new knowledge onto a poster board. You complete drawings that show examples of your information, you clearly label your drawings, you define terms, and you write a well-developed paragraph about the region's contributions to the country. You turn it in and eagerly anticipate the grade, knowing you have demonstrated your learning.

The project grade comes back, and the only points missing are for *coloring*. Yes, coloring. When things like this happen, all we can think of is this: "What learning standard is coloring?" Coloring may add to the overall appearance of a project or assignment, and directions may very well include things such as coloring, but what learning does it represent? Requiring students to create a high-quality visual is not a bad thing, but using a grade to punish the student and "teach" accountability is unproductive. Instead of saying, "Gotcha!" and lowering the grade for not following directions, the teacher could simply advise the student to reread the instructions, complete all requirements, and re-submit.

One thing is certain: This is not the time to lower a grade. Following directions is a *behavior* that we want students to demonstrate, but as established in Cleanse One, behaviors are separate from academic achievement. A grade must be aligned to learning and should accurately measure how well a student has mastered a standard. Including something unrelated to the standards, such as *coloring*, communicates to students and parents an *inaccurate* proficiency level on the assessed standard. According to Dr. Rick Stiggins, a well respected expert on feedback and assessment, "Inaccurate feedback is counter-productive." There should be no surprises for students who engage in instruction, practice, and assessments that are well designed and intentionally aligned to the standards. Alignment is critical to ensure that time spent in the classroom is used efficiently and will elicit the best results for our students.

CHALLENGE ONE

DEVELOP SUMMATIVE ASSESSMENT METHODS FOR EACH STANDARD

Instructions for Required Action Steps

- **Inspect:** Examine the current summative assessment tools.

- **Review:** Revisit the standards and review the student demands.

- **Check:** Compare the standard(s) to the items/tasks on the assessment and check for alignment.

- **Modify:** Adjust the assessment if necessary.

- **Create:** Develop new assessments if necessary to align them with the standards.

Strategy: Examine one summative assessment that you have used in the past year as well as the standards and student-friendly learning targets for that unit of study. If it is a test, go through the items and match them up with the standards and targets. When there is not a clear match, analyze the item. Determine whether the question should be removed or changed. Also pay attention to the *verbs* in the selected standard(s) and make sure the test items are matching the cognitive level to meet the demands of the standard. If the assessment is performance-based, carefully look through the steps in the process that are needed to produce the final product. Does the *product* demonstrate evidence of learning the standard? Does the development process match the learning targets along the way to mastery?

Strategy (student involvement): Students are an asset in designing and constructing summative assessment tools. When they have access to the standards and learning targets and understand what they mean, the *sky's* the limit for what they can produce. When assessing a standard, give your students the standard and have them "prove it." They will come up with ideas that you never would have dreamed of to demonstrate their proficiency.

I incorporated this assessment strategy with my own students in a novice-level Spanish class. The standard asked students to describe different types of foods and beverages using a variety of vocabulary and sentence structures. The students and I broke down the standard (as well as the others for this unit) into meaningful learning targets and worked through the unit of study. The students *owned* the process and chose how they wanted to show evidence of their learning. On the summative assessment, I received a wide variety of submissions ranging from menus with detailed descriptions of the offerings to food journals and restaurant critiques. Most students learned and demonstrated more than the standard demanded and went above and beyond what I expected! The students delighted in the fact that they controlled how they showed their learning. Instead of "Show me the money!" (from the movie *Jerry Maguire*), the catchphrase became "Show me the learning!" The students knew from the outset of the unit that the assessment was *theirs* to *own*, so they prepared their ideas along the way and modified them when necessary.

Beginning with the *end* in mind is a must for standards-aligned units of study. Therefore, we will tackle the summative assessment first. Once the summative assessment is developed and planned, a fluid process is created for planning instruction, crafting learning experiences, and creating formative assessments. The unit of study is exclusively targeted at the end goal. If we start the other way and plan instructional activities first, then create formative assessments, and finally develop the summative assessment, the process is guided by what we taught rather than by what the standards demand. The standards and targets must be in the *driver's seat* so that alignment can be achieved. Again, there should be no surprises for students. They should know what the summative assessment will entail from the beginning of a given unit of study. This not only establishes a clear endpoint and destination for learning, but it also shows students the relevancy of the process by which they learn.

Too many teachers have not had training in crafting quality assessments. They may use textbook-generated assessments because they are *supposed* to be aligned and give a good picture of student understanding. However, textbook assessments are not always as aligned and robust as we would like them to be. Teachers often use these because they feel there is not enough time to develop assessments of their own. This is a *false truth*. Yes, time is precious, but giving a quality assessment that provides true evidence of learning based on the standards is essential. Giving a ready-made assessment without analyzing it for alignment can waste time and send a poisonous "gotcha" message to students. If the assessment does not provide proof of learning the standards, the teacher will have to seek additional evidence and add another assessment. Taking a hard look at ready-made assessments shows that many of them don't address the complexity of the standards. They include *baseline* questions that will only provide *baseline* information. How can we give the highest marks to any of our students when we only have proof of a low-level understanding? These types of assessments are also used because they are easy to score. This dilemma can be fixed when we shorten our assessments and directly target them at the standards. Please be sure you have set yourself free from thinking tests must be 10, 20, 25, or 33 questions worth 10, 5, 4, or 3 points each. Many teachers are still being held prisoners to making sure the number of points per question fits perfectly into the 100-point grading system. Give yourself permission to drastically shorten your tests. There is no need to even give ten low-level questions when three to four well-crafted questions at a higher level will provide enough evidence to determine a proficiency level.

I was working with a middle school teacher who experienced a moment of clarity regarding alignment. She said, "I want to show you something I used a few years ago." She pulled out a test and quickly flipped it to the back side. At the end of the test was an extra credit question: "How old do you think I am?" She started laughing and said, "I can't believe I actually used this!" She told me that she had completely stopped using extra credit and that her current assessments would never include questions that did not align to her standards. We talked about how she had used extra credit to help her students just in case they answered a question incorrectly, but at that point, she had never really taken a hard look at the alignment of her assessments. The best part of this moment was the realization of how far she had come in her practice. Now that her assessments are tightly aligned with the standards, she understands that her new assessments better provide students with the opportunity to show evidence of their learning. She has developed the confidence that her grades mean so much more now than they did before. This example of assessment misalignment may seem extreme, but know that this also happens in subtle ways, including the misinterpretation of the standards, unclear performance criteria, and the inclusion of questions or requirements within the content area that are unrelated to the standard. Close attention must be paid to alignment so that grades accurately reflect learning.

Designing high quality assessments requires teachers to think about what students should do to demonstrate mastery. Teachers should read each standard and consider the following:

- What are the student demands?

- What evidence would show what students know, understand, and are able to do?

- What type of assessment (test, project, written response, presentation, etc.) would best elicit that evidence?

Spending time analyzing current assessments, modifying them as necessary, and crafting new ones when required is indispensable. Without quality assessment tools, we do not have accurate readings of proficiency levels, therefore, we do not have accurate information for reporting. If possible, meet with other teachers to design your summative assessments. Creating four or five questions related to each standard is a good guideline to follow. Everything will make sense to your students if all tasks and items correlate directly with the proficiency levels established in Cleanse Four. Online resources and standardized tests can provide helpful examples in aligning your summative assessments. Do not wait to create your tests. This can be your summer homework, and hopefully, you might have additional time to work on these during a professional development day.

How can we improve our assessments? We know the saying, "Practice makes perfect." Our assessments won't be *perfect*, but they will improve with *practice*. Some have changed this phrase to "Practice makes progress." Keep the standards close by when creating assessments, and reference them often. After administering an assessment, analyze the evidence it gives you.

Answer the following questions:

- Is the evidence what you expected?
- Are you getting the evidence you need to determine a proficiency level on the standard(s)?
- Does the evidence address the standard(s) in sum and not just the smaller targets?

Aligning your summative assessments precisely with the learning targets takes commitment, analysis, and persistent revision. Shorter and more accurate assessment tools, however, will save you a lot of time in the long run. More importantly, student grades (and high school GPAs) will become significantly more meaningful.

Challenge One should give practical steps to ensure that your summative assessment tools are providing accurate evidence of student learning. When that evidence aligns to the standards and students know how to show proficiency, the grading part is easy!

Reflect:

_____

_____

_____

_____

_____

_____

CHALLENGE TWO

CREATE FORMATIVE ASSESSMENTS FOR LEARNING TARGETS, BUILDING UP TO THE STANDARDS

Instructions for Required Action Steps

- **Identify:** Determine the learning targets to be monitored throughout the unit.

- **Analyze:** Review current methods of checking for understanding.

- **Determine:** Decide whether current formative assessment tools (practice/extra practice) are effective and efficient. If not, either make modifications or create something new.

Strategy: Working backward from your summative assessment(s) for a unit, take a close look at the formative assessment tools you have used. Place your learning targets next to you, and analyze the alignment just as you did in Challenge One. If there is misalignment, you may either modify the assessments to align with the learning targets or get rid of the old formative assessment tools and create something new. Ask yourself the following questions: What information do these give me to steer my instruction? What information can my students gather from these to support their learning and understanding of where they are in the process? Am I using a variety of methods to best gauge where my students are?

Strategy (student involvement): Develop a bank of formative practice and assessment tools, and allow the students to choose which ones they would like to do. Students may also create formative assessment tools once the learning targets are understandable to them. This is not recommended at the beginning of a school year. Modeling these tools first is important so that students can develop an understanding of quality formative assessments. After this, the creation of some practice and assessment tools can fall on their shoulders. This actively involves the students in their learning and progress toward mastering the standards.

Provide the students a few guiding questions to create formative assessment and practice tools:

- What are the learning targets for this unit?

- What do the *verbs* ask students to do?

- What types of activities will allow students to practice those *verbs* and *targets*?

- Within the activities, are the questions, items, and prompts appropriate?

Also, provide any resources that may be helpful to the students. These can be online resources, print resources, and even *yourself* as a point-person. Remind them to use each other as resources as well. Throughout this process, students can gain a deep level of proficiency and may feel more prepared for the summative assessment.

Formative assessment tools must be aligned to the learning targets as summative assessments are aligned to the standards. A formative assessment is part of the process by which students learn. Unpacking or deconstructing standards into learning targets makes the standards accessible to students and parents alike. Students can then chart a course for their learning and know if they are on their way to mastering the standards. Using the steps from Cleanse Three, get students on board and invested so that they can *own* these learning targets and their learning.

Quality formative assessments are the key to learning. They inform both the teacher and the student of current proficiency levels on each target and give a clear picture of what is to come. Can you imagine a football coach not knowing where each player is in learning the plays? What about a band director not informing each band member routinely about their current status and specific areas of improvement? Formative assessments not only give a picture of where students are with their learning, but they also set up checkpoints to gauge progress along the way. Teachers already use a variety of formative assessment methods, so let's maximize the value of them and honor practices that are currently in place.

Recognize that if you do the same thing every day, the students will not necessarily be showing you their learning but showing you how they have mastered "the game." Be sure to vary your methods, vary your question styles, and sometimes throw in a *crazy game* to determine mastery.

Providing students with multiple ways to show their progress taps into the variety of ways that kids learn. If we offer them only one way to showcase their knowledge, we may be getting a *false read* on their true level of understanding. This works against student motivation if they feel they know it but can't show it. Kids can write about their learning, talk about their learning, model their learning, create with their learning, etc., and many times students can come up with innovative ways to show what they know, understand, and are able to do. Time is always at a premium, and accurate formative assessment data reclaims time that might have been otherwise spent *grading* or *marking* without a hard look at what the evidence is revealing about student learning. Work smarter, not harder!

Challenge Two should allow you to analyze your formative assessment practices to enhance the learning process. Giving careful thought to how and when you formatively assess will inform both you and your students on how to move forward.

Reflect:

_____

_____

_____

_____

_____

_____

CHALLENGE THREE

ALIGN INSTRUCTION TO SUPPORT STUDENTS ON THE PATHWAY TO LEARNING

Instructions for Required Action Steps

- **Develop:** Craft instructional practices that are standards aligned.

- **Analyze:** Identify the type of data or information each formative assessment provides.

- **Modify:** Adjust instruction along the way to meet student needs.

Strategy: Start with your _comfort zone_ and think about a normal class period. How do you instruct students? Do you lean toward whole group, small group, or individualized instruction? Is the classroom more teacher-centered or student-centered? Who is doing most of the work? Now, think about all your assessment practices and how they fit into the instructional progression of a unit of study.

Strategy (student involvement): Survey your students at the beginning of the year about their preferences regarding instruction and environment. This can be done very simply by using a *forced choice* activity. Have students move to the part of the room which corresponds with their answer to the question. Some sample questions include the following:

- Do you prefer pencil/paper or digital practice?

- Do you prefer whole group, small group, or individualized instruction?

- When practicing, do you prefer to work in a small group or on your own?

- Do you function best in a quiet room or with some noise?

This is a quick, effective way to gauge the best ways to reach your students. When doing this in my classroom, I was always surprised at the differences that appeared throughout the day. I thought I would notice quite a few similarities between classes, but that is not what happened. Some classes really wanted time to work together as they learned while others wanted a more individualized setting. There were others that were split on this particular question. The beauty in knowing more about how your students prefer to learn is that you can not only work to meet their needs, but you can also review their preferences with them when things are not working so well and make changes as necessary.

Student preferences may push you out of your *wheelhouse* as a teacher, but giving students some choice and ownership promotes investment and a strong feeling of "we are in this together." When the idea is that "we" build the environment together, everyone's wishes can be honored from time to time, including the teacher's. Don't forget that while student choices are important, at times the teacher will have to step in and make some of these decisions. For example, having a completely silent room or a noisy one every day is not feasible or beneficial. Be clear with your students that you will make the call when necessary, and at other times, you will work to give them their preferences. Remind students that when the room is quiet, some students thrive, and for those who would like a little more noise, there is a time for that as well. There are also many opportunities to have several of the choices going on at the same time. For example, the students who prefer more noise could utilize headphones to listen to music, while those who prefer the quiet could work silently without disruption.

Aligning instruction to support student learning also involves looking at the standards and the skills that will be demonstrated at the end of the unit. As you plan, keep in mind that setting a rigid instructional plan, with certain topics locked into certain days on the calendar, does not necessarily meet the needs of your students. You will want to include formative assessments which will shed light on your students' needs for next steps, whether they are prepared and ready to move on or need some reteaching and clarification. Creating an overall plan that keeps in mind the importance of flexibility is a plan for student learning rather than a plan for completion. Many teachers have curriculum maps that provide structure but feel restrictive. Teachers feel that if they are not "on pace" with the map, they are doing a disservice to their students. This is not true unless the readiness of the students matches the pacing of the map. Teaching is *responsive*. To maximize instruction and learning, we must find out as much as possible about the proficiency of our students through formative assessments. When teachers respond to a *map* or *guide* rather than to the students *sitting before them*, they run the risk of disengagement, frustration, and complacency.

"As a beginning teacher, I was given the curriculum maps for my department and told to use them. I interpreted this as my pacing Bible and did not feel that I could stray from it and be an effective teacher. The map included not only time frames

for student learning but also the topics to be covered and instructional strategies for each. With this as a guide, I did not refer back to my standards when planning instruction. I also did not consider my learners when doing this planning. Over time, I realized that I could improve my planning, and more importantly, my instruction by paying more attention to those two things rather than the map itself. The map was still important—I knew that there would a be common assessment at the end of the marking period. I was responsible for preparing my students for these assessments, but my thinking had changed regarding how to go about this. Instead of starting with the map, I started with the standards and my students. I looked at the learning targets, what they demanded of my students, and where my students were with their proficiency. This change had a huge impact on my effectiveness as an instructor."

-Kirk Humphreys, Mathematics Instructor, Deerfield, IL

Continual pairing of the learning goals and formative-assessment evidence gives that laser sharp focus to classroom experiences. The instruction that comes out of this process maintains the clarity of aligned summative and formative assessment processes. Utilizing tools such as curriculum maps will support the process, but these are only *support* tools. They are not the *end all be all*—rather, they are part of the means to the end.

Challenge Three should re-emphasize the importance of alignment regarding instruction. Pairing evidence of formative assessment with instructional decision making maintains an active focus on learning in the classroom. Responding to student needs while still attending to the goals and objectives laid out in a curriculum guide or map is where teaching becomes *art* rather than *science*. If you create a safe instructional environment where everyone has the same goal, it works!

Reflect:

_____

_____

_____

_____

_____

_____

CHALLENGE FOUR

GIVE OWNERSHIP OF THE LEARNING PROCESS TO STUDENTS THROUGH PRACTICE

Instructions for Required Action Steps

- **Gather:** Compile a list of the various types of practice opportunities in your classroom.

- **Sort:** Organize practice opportunities in a logical order of progression or separated by skill.

- **Reflect:** Answer the following questions: Which are most effective? Why do they work well?

- **Decide:** Identify which practice activities are non-negotiable and which are optional.

- **Create:** Develop a structure to build *student choice* into the process.

Strategy: Look at all the *practice* assignments and activities in a unit of study. Put the assignments and activities in order of progression with the learning targets. Consider the following questions as you examine the unit:

- Would every student need to complete all assignments or activities to achieve proficiency? The short answer is *no*.

- When looking at these practice opportunities, do you see any that are non-negotiable and need to be completed by all students to demonstrate where their learning is in relation to the standard?

- Are there some that are not vital to every student? The answer here is most likely *yes*.

Deciding which assignments and activities are non-negotiable and which are optional is an important step in providing student choice. Once identified, decisions about those optional activities can be given over to the students.

Strategy (student involvement): For a given unit, gather some *sample* assignments that students could complete. Put the students in groups and ask them to organize the assignments. They can choose to put them into a learning progression or categorize them in some other way. Have each group share their organizational strategy and reasoning for using it. Next, have students rate the activities from *most* to *least* helpful in their learning. Ask them to consider what the activity is having them do. Are they writing? Speaking? Doing something hands on? This is essential feedback for the teacher moving forward.

There are many ways to give ownership to students through *practice* in the classroom. Tic-tac-toe boards, learning contracts, choice boards, and many other options put students in the *driver's seat* to make decisions about their learning. When providing these choices for students, teachers must develop a *bank* of quality assignments and activities that are closely aligned to the standards.

For veteran teachers, these banks are more easily constructed. They have had access, over the years, to a wide variety of resources and have also had the time to create many of their own practice activities. They have had time to collaborate with colleagues to develop these assignment banks as well as to vet the assignments for quality and effectiveness. For newer teachers, these collaborative experiences are critical. Teaching is not a profession that should be practiced in isolation. Newer teachers need to be able to rely on their colleagues for resources and insight developed over their years in the classroom. At the same time, veteran staff can learn a lot from newer teachers as they bring a fresh perspective to what quality assignments look like and entail.

Once a bank of quality, aligned assignments and activities has been developed for a unit of study, teachers can decide when allowing *student choice* would be appropriate. Student choice can be as simple as two practice options to choose from or a larger bank of assignments. As a teacher, you know your students. Reflect on how many choices would be beneficial to them. If a large bank of assignments and activities would distract from the learning, a smaller one would be more appropriate. The idea is to have *student choice* supporting *student learning*. With clear alignment of assignments and activities and built-in student choice, the process of learning becomes a powerful *intrinsic motivator*. Students are involved in the process and know where they are now, where they want to be, and how they plan to get there.

Challenge Four should help you think about student involvement in selecting and constructing practice activities. Students will be very honest with you when asked how useful some assignments are in helping them learn. Teachers that collaborate with their fellow academic team members and take the students' ideas into consideration have a much better chance of developing high-quality assessments. Do not be afraid to reinvent yourself and your lessons, and keep reminding yourself to take *baby steps* to keep from being overwhelmed.

Reflect:

_____

_____

_____

_____

_____

Dr. Anne Davies is an author, consultant, and researcher with expertise that correlates perfectly with Cleanse Five. In *Ahead of the Curve*, she explains:

> "*Research shows that when students are involved in the assessment process they learn more, achieve at higher levels, and are more motivated. When evaluative feedback (letter grade, number grade, etc.) is decreased, and specific, descriptive feedback is increased, students learn more.*"

CLEANSE NUMBER SIX
CAN I USE A CONSISTENT FEEDBACK
PROCESS TO MAXIMIZE STUDENT GROWTH?

"Students can learn without grades, but they can't learn without descriptive, timely feedback."

-Rick Wormeli

Feedback is the *sweet spot* in learning. The ebb and flow of finding out what students know and can do, paired with conversation about next steps, creates a loop that is critical in learning. Maintaining consistency with feedback or utilizing a common method for both giving and receiving feedback spurs confidence and motivation. When feedback is consistent and ongoing, students don't get "stuck" for long amounts of time. Their success *snowballs* as they "move up a level" in the learning process. Motivation soars for students, and the belief that **they can and will achieve** spreads like wildfire. When there are setbacks along the road to success, feedback gets students moving again. Increasing the amount of quality feedback for students, while reducing the amount of grading, communicates that learning is of utmost importance.

Are grades feedback? Some will argue that the answer to this question is *yes*. In their traditional form, however, grades are not feedback. Even when grades are cleansed, they are quite limited in what they can tell us about specific student proficiencies. On the other hand, grades are important because they can impact course placement, college acceptance, athletic eligibility, scholarship money, and more. As a result, focusing on the accuracy of grades is imperative. Our goal of *maximizing student learning* and a*ccurate reporting* requires a laser sharp focus on the feedback we are providing students.

If grades help determine class placement, they must *mean* something about academic proficiency. How many times have students been placed in higher-level coursework because they played the *game of school* well? Conversely, how many times have students been placed in lower-level coursework because of poor work habits? Good work habits are essential, but placing these students in lower-level classes will not automatically improve those behaviors. This could, in fact, further deter them from showing good citizenship because their *academic readiness* is not being honored. Are you ready to improve student behavior and increase academic achievement? Model the behavior you seek from students, and give actionable feedback for next steps.

In his article, "Forget Big Goals. Take Baby Steps for Small Daily Wins," performance specialist, John Brubaker, says: "Small daily progress is a powerful motivator." Consistent feedback will maximize student growth because it establishes the opportunity for students to experience "small daily wins" in the learning process using the power of momentum. Don't miss this important opportunity to instill in students how to manufacture momentum by *knowing* they are making progress. According to Brubaker, "Psychologists say the closer we get to a goal, the harder we are willing to work to achieve the goal." Expert financial planner, Dave Ramsey, calls this the "Snowball Effect," which clients experience when they take a *baby step* in paying off one credit card, then another, then another until the power of *momentum* takes over and they are debt free. Our students need healthy, consistent feedback to experience "small daily wins" or incremental *baby steps* of improvement to control their own satisfaction and motivation. Learning is a motivator, so trust it!

In his research on various teaching practices and their impact on student learning, John Hattie concluded that when teachers use words to give students clear feedback about how they are performing on a standard, the results are amazing. In his book, *Visible Learning*, he shares a collection of evidence-based research that shows what actually works in schools to improve learning. One of the most powerful conclusions, resulting from 7,827 studies on learning and instruction, is that when teachers provide specific information about a student's standing (not a grade from the 100-point system) in terms of a specific standard, achievement increased by 37%. The most powerful single indicator that enhances achievement is feedback (using words).

Over the years in my classroom, my feedback methods changed drastically. In the beginning, I truly did not place enough emphasis on the importance of feedback. I relied on the age-old belief that grades play a big role in student improvement. When I did give feedback, it was not very effective. I used vague written comments like "Good job!" or "That's incorrect." I had stickers that said the same things, so those could also replace my handwritten comments on an assessment. I was missing a huge opportunity to improve student learning and get to know my students on an entirely new level. When feedback becomes an ongoing conversation between the student and teacher, relationships build. The result is an act of *working together* to achieve, and students no longer feel as if they are left to *figure it out* on their own.

With time, my feedback methods improved. However, at first, I spent way too much time on feedback. I wrote paragraphs (yes, multiple paragraphs) on each student's assessment to make sure I was addressing his or her strengths and areas for growth. Although strengths and areas for growth make for effective feedback, there is no need to write multiple paragraphs on each assessment. Eventually, I developed a method where I highlighted what the student did in relation to the standard and then identified next steps in their learning. I could provide feedback in a sentence or two (written or verbal). The time spent providing feedback was reduced significantly, and the time it took students to read and interpret the feedback decreased as well.

"It is not hard to learn more. What is hard is to unlearn when you discover yourself wrong."

-Martin H. Fisher

CHALLENGE ONE

GIVE YOURSELF PERMISSION TO GRADE LESS

Instructions for Required Action Steps

- **Determine:** Identify which assignments in your classroom are graded.
- **Analyze:** Do they all need to be graded, or are there opportunities for giving feedback only?
- **Analyze:** Could the students check their responses themselves?
- **Try It!** This can be difficult, but the results are worth it!

Strategy: Find one *practice* assignment that you have typically graded in the past. Maybe it is a homework assignment or something completed in class. Ask yourself, "Why did I grade this in the past?" If you are unsure, or if the reason is that you wanted students to complete the assignment, then a grade is not necessary. The purpose of grading is not student management. If you are thinking, "if I don't grade it, they won't do it," please know that our Power of ICU schools often have 100% assignment completion with drastically less grading. Students will realize a sense of urgency to complete assignments when the consequence is to complete them on *their* time. Be sure you also explain the importance and relevancy of the assignment to your students. You may be surprised with the result.

Strategy (student involvement): Students may arrive to our classrooms conditioned to look for a grade on every assignment. They may also be conditioned to ask how many points assignments are worth from the outset, so grading less can be a significant transition for everyone in the classroom. Ask students if grades are essential to learn. At first, they may say *yes*, but if you probe further, they will see the disconnect between grading and learning. Ask them if there are some assignments where having a letter or a number at the top would not matter. There will be kids that still resist the process, but allow them the time and space to make the change. Reiterate the importance of how quality feedback supports learning much more than a letter or number.

Early in my teaching career, I was under the impression that *everything* must be graded. I believed that students wouldn't do assignments unless they were graded and that grading everything gave the assignments *weight* and *importance*. I presumed that putting a score at the top of a page gave students valuable feedback. Today, I know none of that is true. Students will do the work and give their best effort even when they know it will not be graded. My students actually produced higher quality work once the grades disappeared on their formative work. The students were still doing as much as they were before, but they were doing it without the fear of being perfect every time they tried something.

This was not something, however, that happened overnight. My students had been conditioned to value only the work that was graded. This is a *teacher* problem, not a *student* one. When teachers consistently assign point values to assignments, talk with students about how much they can earn, and hold this over the students' heads when assigning and grading the work, the problem persists. When teachers cleanse their grading practices and communicate with students about the changes and why they are happening, students will make the shift as well.

What took the place of the grades? Feedback. Meaningful, powerful, timely feedback. My time was not spent calculating numbers, percentages, weights, and letters. As difficult as this may sound, **give yourself permission to grade less**. You are not decreasing the importance of an assignment by not grading it. You have decided that learning is valued over grades and are willing to show that to your students. You are replacing the time spent figuring out point values and algorithms with time to dispense quality feedback.

Challenge One may feel uncomfortable for many teachers. The time-honored practice of grading *everything* has been challenged. However, this challenge should also provide a sense of freedom for you and your students. You can *let go* of some of the time you spend grading and analyzing grades with your students, and you can replace that time with a greater focus on student learning and effective feedback.

Reflect:

_____

_____

_____

_____

_____

_____

CHALLENGE TWO

DEVELOP AN UNDERSTANDING OF WHAT QUALITY FEEDBACK LOOKS LIKE FOR STUDENTS

Instructions for Required Action Steps

- **Understand:** Determine the characteristics of quality feedback.

- **Analyze:** Discern the difference between feedback that does not move student learning forward and feedback (advice) that supports learning and student ownership.

Strategy: With colleagues, develop a list of advice that you give students to move forward with learning. Use the word *advice* at this time rather than the word *feedback* which is often muddied with *grades*. Using this list, discuss the effectiveness of the advice and what student action would look like when that advice is given. Teachers often look at feedback and advice differently, but they should mirror each other. Create a list of the characteristics that make the advice effective.

Strategy (student involvement): Create some note cards with a variety of situations familiar to students, such as the following: You are struggling in math class, you are having a difficult time getting along with a friend, there is a particular piece of music that you are having a tough time mastering, etc. Hand out the cards to students and have them write a piece of advice for the situation. Then talk as a class about the advice given, the effectiveness of the advice, and the ways in which students might respond or act upon the advice.

The word *advice* signifies that you are helping someone move forward. Whether the purpose is to help someone face a tough situation or solve a difficult problem, the goal of advice is for the person to have an idea of how to proceed. When asked for advice, people naturally think of next steps. On the other hand, feedback can wrongly be seen as a time for teachers to simply *comment* on what was done without giving advice on how to move forward. Feedback should be *meaningful* and *actionable*. It should move learning forward, not just give a reflection on what was already done.

The reality is, there is good advice and bad advice out there. This is also true of feedback, so be mindful of that when talking with students. With good feedback, the road ahead is clear, and students know where they are headed and what success looks like when they get there. When cleansing grading practices, remember that an important step is to **grade less** and **give more feedback** so that the focus for students is on learning. Quality feedback ensures quality learning.

Challenge Two should pair the idea of giving someone good advice to providing quality feedback on student work. Effective feedback must guide and lead students forward. If students don't act on the feedback they are getting, time to change your practice!

Reflect:

_____

_____

_____

_____

_____

CHALLENGE THREE

DETERMINE A METHOD FOR GIVING FEEDBACK TO STREAMLINE THE PROCESS

Instructions for Required Action Steps

- **Identify:** Determine essential elements/steps necessary for quality feedback.

- **Develop:** Create action steps for giving quality feedback for teacher and student use.

- **Teach:** Show students how to give and receive quality feedback.

Strategy: Meet with another teacher and talk about specific times when you were given feedback as a student. Discuss when it was effective and when it felt as if it had zero impact on learning. Identify the elements of the feedback that had the biggest impact on you as a learner, and then reflect on your own practice.

Strategy (student involvement): Make a list of various comments that teachers would normally write on student assignments. Ask students to discuss what the feedback tells them and what the next steps would be based upon the feedback. Provide a variety of feedback from the non-descriptive "Good job" and "Needs work" to much more specific words such as, "You have provided the textual evidence. How could you tie it to your claim?" Students may never have thought much about the feedback provided to them by teachers, but this process will shed some light on how feedback can make the next steps clear for students.

Feedback must be *specific* and *timely*. For some students, there is a need for feedback on multiple learning targets, and for others, there may be just one area that needs improvement. If multiple errors and misunderstandings exist on an assignment or assessment, choose a focus area and give feedback on that first. Let the student see the focus of the feedback, and tell him or her that any additional areas for improvement will be targeted in the future. This does two things for students. First, they will have a clear awareness of the error or misunderstanding. Second, they will have a clear starting point. They will know what to do and how to progress. When multiple areas for improvement are indicated with quite a bit of feedback, students can feel overwhelmed and won't know where to begin. Remember, taking a *baby step* toward a goal is an intrinsic motivator, so break it down for them. This practice is also a time saver for teachers, as it allows them to put less feedback on each paper and get assignments and assessments back into the hands of students in a timely fashion. This has a huge impact. Can you remember a time when you got a paper back two weeks after you turned it in? Did the feedback lead to more learning at that point? Even if it did, the impact is lower. Many times the length of time it takes to get feedback to students corresponds to its impact on learning. When the elapsed time increases, the impact decreases unless the teacher has determined that a slight delay would be beneficial for the student to figure out an error on their own. This is not to say that the quality of the feedback should suffer because of timeliness. Taking an additional day to ensure that the feedback moves student learning forward is well worth the time for the teacher and the wait for the students.

To maximize efficiency, develop a method or system to give students feedback. You want to give them as much feedback as possible within reason. Before I had a systematic way to communicate feedback to my students, I spent much more time on it than was needed.

There are three major components to quality feedback:

1. Identify the target.
2. Communicate where the student is in relation to that target.
3. Map out the next steps.

Feedback such as "Good Job" or "Excellent Work" does not move learning forward. This feedback is well intentioned but not centered on improving student learning—missing all three of the major components. The intention of that style of feedback is to make a student feel good about his or her work. The problem is that there is no information to support the student with next steps. What do they mean? Is "Good Job" telling me that I am proficient and ready to delve more deeply? Is it telling me that I am progressing well but have room to grow to meet the standard? When students see feedback like this, it is a *stop sign*. The work is good enough, and they are done with it. The students view this type of feedback as an *endpoint* to learning and signal to move on to the next topic. When students achieve proficiency, we do want them to move on, but we also want them to see the connections to previous learning. We don't want learning to feel compartmentalized—it should be a continuum.

Challenge Three should encourage you to use the *three components* for effective feedback: identifying the target, communicating where the student is in relation to that target, and mapping out the next steps. Using these, create a model for giving effective feedback to your students. Advising students on the next steps in their learning should be on the top of every teacher's mind, every day.

Reflect:

_____

_____

_____

_____

CHALLENGE FOUR

USE YOUR FEEDBACK METHOD NOT ONLY FOR YOURSELF, BUT ALSO WITH THE STUDENTS

TEACH THEM TO SELF-ASSESS AND GIVE FEEDBACK TO PEERS

Instructions for Required Action Steps

- **Demonstrate:** Model the feedback method to be used in class.
- **Practice:** Utilize the method with the students.
- **Facilitate:** Guide students to self-assess with this method.
- **Provide:** Create opportunities for students to give feedback to peers using this method.

Strategy: Try the step-by-step method for giving students feedback from Challenge Three. Before trying this with students, do a practice round with a colleague. Find a *student work sample* and provide some feedback using the method you created. Ask your colleague what he or she would do next. Is the response what you expected? Consider how long providing the feedback takes you. Is the method concise enough to use with a larger quantity of students?

Strategy (student involvement): Students can become involved in the feedback method once it is modeled by their teacher and they have had ample opportunities to practice. After the feedback method is modeled for students, give them an old work sample (preferably from a prior school year) and ask them to give feedback to their peers.

Their peers can then evaluate whether or not it provides clear *next steps*. This is also a great activity for students to see what proficiency looks like (and what it does *not* look like) for a standard they are currently working on.

Developing a method for giving quality feedback saves time for both students and teachers. Teachers will become experienced with the process and be able to produce quality comments more easily and effectively. Students will understand the method as well and be able to interpret the feedback quickly and turn it into action. Feedback methods are also effective for student self-assessment. Many times, students are very hard on themselves when asked to self-assess because they tend to be *judgment* based. That is, they focus on if it is *good* or *bad*. Once students learn to identify how the work relates to the standard(s) and indicate next steps, the assessment of the work improves.

Getting my students to understand and use the feedback method took some time. The explanation of the process is simple, but putting it into practice is more difficult. I consistently reminded students of the process by saying, "Here is what you did, here is how it relates to our learning targets, and now I would like you to do this." For example, "This paragraph addresses and communicates your personal likes and dislikes, which are two of our learning targets. Looking ahead, I would like you to write about likes and dislikes for another person." Once the students could understand, interpret, and put the feedback into action, they were ready to try it. The students became proficient in identifying the relationships between the work and the targets, but at times, determining the *next steps* was still difficult for them. This is when stepping in to support my students was important. Eventually my students became successful with that last step, but getting there took practice. The best thing about using the method for peer and self-assessment was that the judgment of *good* or *bad* was left out of the conversation. Students began discussing their level of proficiency in relation to the standards and where they needed to go from there.

Challenge Four should encourage you to share the process of giving feedback with your students. Peer-to-peer interaction and feedback can be one of the most effective means of learning. The idea is to make your classroom and your students self-sufficient. Teachers do not need to take on the large task of giving feedback alone. Students can *own* part of the process. Be the *guiding* force in your classroom, but not the *driving* force.

Reflect:

_____

_____

_____

_____

_____

_____

Because feedback is the cornerstone of student learning, we *must* get it right. A *letter* or *number* does not provide adequate information for a student to move forward. At best, it is a quick reflection of what *was* with no information on what *will be*. Providing quality feedback to students signals that learning is continuous. We are never stopping, just pausing to evaluate current progress and to make decisions about where to go next. With all this in mind, teachers must focus on providing this valuable feedback. We cannot spend every waking moment outside of class on feedback, so our method for giving feedback must be efficient. Keeping our language tied to the standards and focused on where to go next gets rid of the *extra language* that makes giving feedback a more time-intensive process.

CONCLUSION
CHASING RABBITS

Have you heard the story of the farmer who sent his son to prepare a field? The father *simplified* how to till straight lines by telling him, "Select an object on the far side of the field, and plow straight at it."

Later, when the father checked his son's progress, there wasn't one straight line. In fact, the lines looked as if the boy had meandered aimlessly without a set goal. Every row was wavy. "I thought I told you to select an object and plow toward it," the father said. "I did, the boy replied, "but the rabbit kept hopping."

For many of my thirty-seven years in education, I was handed the latest federal, state, and/or local initiatives and told to plow toward them. I can go all the way back to 1978, my eighth and ninth grade science teaching days, to share the respective *object* I was told to progress toward. I was handed a different colored booklet of objectives (at one point called standards, another point called goals) every four years to *re-direct* me to the *promised land*. And the rabbit kept hopping…

"No Child Left Behind", "more emphasis on PE", "no more cupcakes for birthdays", "more emphasis on history", and "if every student will read at least one hour per day, then we can compete with China" are a few that come to mind. Think about the recent emphasis on test scores, Common Core Standards, and RTI, and ask yourselves, "Will these hop around also?" Of course, they will.

They already are, and the aimless meandering toward constantly moving objects is *wearing out* teachers and administrators. We cannot control what next *quick-fix* initiative will be handed down, but we can stop *chasing the rabbits*. Student learning is our main purpose, so fixate on it and plow straight toward it.

Grade Cleanse is a six-step process to uncover what lies within traditional grading practices so that you can reflect, make changes, and improve. We encourage you to move at your own pace, taking one cleanse at a time and moving to the next cleanse only when you are ready. Take *baby steps*, but don't stop plowing in a straight line toward student learning! The culture of your classroom or school will never be the same, and *intrinsic motivation* will be the norm, not a lofty goal. Grading can be a meaningful process that supports reflection and growth, rather than penalizing students. Accuracy with grading is within reach.

We are convinced our grading cleanse will motivate you and recharge your *teacher battery*. Cleansed grades are healthy grades, and healthy grades support learning.

APPENDIX
HYBRID CONVERSION IDEAS

But My District Still Uses a Traditional Report Card?

Many teachers tell us they know the traditional 0-100 grading scale is unhealthy. These same teachers often say, "I see the benefits of standards-based grading, but my district will most likely never change our traditional report card because our parents would be too upset." Will report cards ever change to reflect each learning standard? Instead of waiting to find out, take control of the things you can control to make your grades healthier. Many teachers discover their own way to convert the daily use of learning levels into a 0-100 number grade. For the purpose of this book, we will refer to these three examples as *Hybrid Conversions* using the following four learning levels:

Mastered (4)

Approaching (3)

On-Track (2)

Below (1)

*LOE (Lack of Evidence) should be used with all conversions to eliminate the most unhealthy part of the 100 point scale which is the 0-59 or 0-69 grades that devastate student motivation and learning. The "No Zero's" discussion simply fades into the past!

HYBRID CONVERSION ONE

In the example below, the "student friendly learning targets" are placed in spaces across the top, student names down the sides, then the exact number correct in the correlating boxes. The denominator (mastery) is the possible number correct and the numerator is the number the student got correct.

One teacher who shifted to this conversion said, "I felt like I was let out of prison. My assessments are much shorter now and standard specific. Making out more than one test is much easier because the number of questions do not have to be divisible by 100!"

With every assessment, correlate the number correct with each of the learning levels and be sure to use LOE (Lack of Evidence) or leave the box blank if the student is *not there* yet.

Grade Book 1st Period MATH 1st 9-Weeks	8/15 Learning Target/Standard	8/16 Learning Target/Standard	8/22 Learning Target/Standard	8/31 Learning Target/Standard	9/1 Learning Target/Standard	9/12 Learning Target/Standard	9/15 Learning Target/Standard	9/16 Learning Target/Standard	Learning Target in Student Friendly Language		
Mastery	12	21	7	17	6	8	11	8			
Valentine Below	10	20	6	14	5	8	10				
Tyesha Langone	10	19	7	17	5	8	11	7			
Marybelle Emily		21		14	6	8	9	7			
Alda Griese	12	18	5	15	5	7	11	7			
Hai Swarts	11	18	5	14	6	8	10	7			
Ralph Moses	11	18	6	17	6	8		8			
Beatriz Warnke	12	21	5	15	5	7	11	7			
Bettie Avera	11	20	6	16	6	8	11	7			

Remember, traditional report cards will force you to still come up with one single number that is a result of averaging all of the numbers for a particular *subject* rather than a specific *standard*.

HYBRID CONVERSION TWO

This formula provides for a more specific *transposed* numeric grade and correlating letter grade. The numbers may need to be adjusted for your district's letter grade ranges.

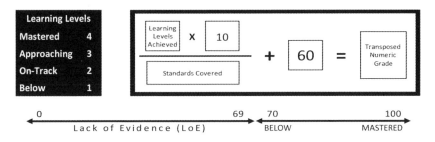

Sample Calculations: SBG Learning Levels to Numeric Grade

	Standards							Learning Levels Achieved	Transposed Numeric Grade	Letter Grade
	1	2	3	4	5	6	7			
Student R	4	4	4	4	4	4	4	28	100	A
Student S	3	3	3	3	4	4	4	24	94	A
Student T	3	3	3	3	3	3	3	21	90	B
Student U	2	2	2	3	3	3	3	18	86	B
Student V	2	2	2	2	2	2	2	14	80	C
Student W	1	1	1	2	2	2	2	11	76	C
Student X	1	1	1	1	2	2	2	10	74	D
Student Y	1	1	1	1	1	1	1	7	70	D
Student Z*	LoE	LoE	LoE	1	1	1	1	4	I	I

*A numeric grade cannot be reported when there is lack of evidence (LOE) of learning. If there is still LOE at the end of a grading period, the teacher may decide to report the grade as "Incomplete" or assign a numeric grade via a separate "Lack of Evidence Alternative Grade Form." If evidence that the student has moved up learning levels for a respective standard is later presented, the teacher may make adjustments as needed to the reported grade.

HYBRID CONVERSION THREE

If your district uses letter grades, then you attach a number from the one hundred point scale with the learning level that fits best. In the sample below, the 60 in this conversion chart represents the lowest passing grade for the district. The numbers should be adjusted if your district uses 70 as the lowest passing grade. Use common sense to adjust all numbers. One high school teacher uses 95 for mastered (but allows students to meet with her if they are dead set on 100), 87 for approaching, 79 for on-track, and 70 for below.

100 for Mastered

90 for Approaching

75 for On-Track

60 for Below

ABOUT THE AUTHORS

Danny Hill

Danny Hill is a nationally respected authority on student apathy and school culture. He has taught science, economics, history, health, and coached football and basketball. He served four years as a high school assistant principal in charge of student management and curriculum. Danny was appointed principal of Southside, a large K-8 school, where  he remained for twenty years. Under his leadership, Southside grew into a highly respected school that enjoyed a positive reputation with the faculty, students, parents, and community.

Danny has presented to over a million educators across the United States and is also a motivational speaker, teacher, author, and educational consultant. He cofounded and is chief manager of Power of ICU. He and his wife and family live in Middle Tennessee.

Garnet Hillman

Garnet Hillman is a nationally recognized educational consultant and author who has extensively researched and implemented standards based learning, assessment, and grading on a classroom and district-wide level. She spent three years as an instructional coach and fifteen years in the classroom as a World Language instructor in the  Chicago area prior to shifting to full-time consulting. Garnet has worked with educators around the country and presented at a variety of conferences—opening minds to the possibilities of a shift to healthier grading practices. She provides a practical approach to establish grading and assessment practices that support learning. Garnet is also a co-moderator of the weekly standards based learning chat (#sblchat) on Twitter.

In her free time, Garnet can be found spending time with her husband, Shawn, and supporting her two sons, Julian and Jackson, on the soccer field. She and her family live in the southwest suburbs of Chicago.

OTHER TITLES AVAILABLE
FROM THE POWER OF ICU LEARNING LIBRARY

Power of ICU

This book takes the reader through the creation of ICU...Intensive Care Unit, from its inception in the classrooms and hallways of schools that resulted in "Every Student Completing Every Assignment." You will hear a practical approach, created by teachers, of how to have all students complete their assignments and create a healthy school culture focused on student learning and accountability. Administrators say *Power of ICU* is excellent for staff book studies because it challenges traditional paradigms and poor educational practices.

Brick House

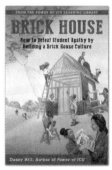

This book provides details for building an infrastructure that pulls together proven educational practices under one roof and outlines the Power of ICU proven formula: Assignment Completion + Quality Assignments + Healthy Grading Practices = Student Success. *Brick House* is not a "quick fix" that is here one day and gone the next. Danny Hill lays the foundation for a culture in which schools rally around student success and improved learning. Students' walls at home may be cracked or broken, but their walls at school can be Brick House strong.